A Kung-Fu Master's Journey

The Life and Martial Arts Experiences of an Asian American

By Allen J. Chinn

A Kung-Fu Master's Journey

All rights reserved.

Copyright ©2009 Allen J. Chinn

This book may not be reproduced, transmitted, or stored in whole or in part by any means, including graphic, electronic, or mechanical without the express written consent of the publisher except in the case of brief quotations embodied in critical articles and reviews.

The photographs seen in this book, are from Allen J. Chinn's personal collection.

ISBN: 978-0-557-11572-3

Published in the United States of America by Lulu.com.

Visit www.akungfumasters.com

Forward

While it is easy to speak to Allen Chinn's exceptional fighting ability and skill with forms; his mastery of ancient and modern weapons, or his talent for teaching that has earned him a well deserved position of respect and esteem in the Pacific Northwest, only his students and close friends can best tell you of his great generosity of time, talent and spirit.

Those who have been recipients of that generosity will probably even tell you that he is often generous to the proverbial fault. He doesn't market or sell his martial art. Instead he passes it on to those who wish to learn with one simple rule: you must put in the time and effort and do the work to get the most out of it.

It is a simple rule really and one that many who come to the martial arts overlook in favor of flash or mystic ceremony. Kung-Fu Master Chinn offers substance with style that is the hallmark of the Chinese fighting arts.

After 20 plus years of covering the Mixed Martial Arts for a variety of national and international martial arts publications I have had the good fortune of getting to know Allen Chinn and with this book you now have that opportunity as well.

He is a gifted martial artist, a true Kung-Fu Master, and I'm proud to say, a loyal friend.

Kregg P.J. Jorgenson

Preface

This book describes my 45 years of martial arts experience and the influences that helped shape me. It is often stated that it is the journey and not the destination that is important.

In a time when little was known about Kung-Fu, and there were few choices to learn any Chinese martial art, I desired to learn. I've seen the growth of Kung Fu over the years, from being a complete secret into so much of mainstream media. Its progress has been impressive to witness.

This book gives insight into my experience as a martial artist, but also describes what it was like growing up as an Asian American in South Seattle's Beacon Hill. In one sense I was just another kid growing up and doing something that he loved.

This book demonstrates that if you desire something enough, you can achieve it. Even against many odds, success is a product of desire, dedication and perseverance. You can overcome ADD/HD, language, bigotry, loss of family members, loss of relationships and insecurities.

I have learned that life is full of twists and turns, and the only constant is change. We don't always know what we will be. I never would have believed that I would be a leader in Seattle's martial arts community and that I would reach this high level of Kung-Fu prowess. I also would never have believed that my personal life would be filled with so many ups and downs.

Our history is the only thing engraved in stone. It can never be changed and the only thing we can do is try to understand it. The future is full of mystery and though we can make educated guesses, none of us know what is to come.

We can only somewhat control our present lives. It is something that we must embrace and accept. As best we can we must understand that our decisions and actions will have effect on our future and those around us. Tomorrow soon becomes today and today quickly becomes yesterday.

We should have the proper mindset to live a good life, make positive decisions, and live our lives without regrets.

* I wrote this book dividing my life experiences and personal thoughts into topic areas. I believed this is easier to follow than chronological order. This topic based writing will also make it easier to refer back to specific areas.

* **Names of people, and/or organizations have been purposely omitted to keep their identity confidential.**

DEDICATION

To my parents whom I will always love and cherish and whom I cannot ever fully repay.

To Susan and Wally for being the wonderful people that they are, and always being there for me.

To Jason and Brandon, my hope and my happiness.

SPECIAL THANKS

Robert Simon Siegel, Lynette Smith and Melissa Chow for editing.

Kregg P. J. Jorgenson, Jason Chinn, Shawn Miller, Renee Ragaza-Miller, Michael Gibson, Alan Trang, and Will Butler for their help with reviewing.

Melissa Chow for graphics assistance.

Susan and Wally Lee for family photographs.

Larry Oliver, Kregg P.J. Jorgenson, Connie L. Chinn, Renee Ragaza-Miller, Martin Kral and numerous others for photography.

TABLE OF CONTENTS

Forward	page 3
Preface	page 4
Dedication, Special Thanks	page 5
Table of Contents	page 6
The Beginning	page 8
The Three Greatest Influences In My Life	page 9
How I Started In Kung-Fu	page 14
Training Under My Father and Alone	page 15
Growing Up	page 19
Early Equipment	page 26
First Uniforms	page 28
ADD/ADHD	page 28
Childhood Heroes	page 29
Wanting to Become a Kung-Fu Instructor	page 30
The 1970s and the Kung-Fu Craze	page 31
The Path of Least Resistance	page 45
Total Peace, or Total War	page 46
My Early Fears	page 48
Mean People Who Thought They Knew Kung-Fu	page 49
1974-1975 Creation of Yee Jong Kune Do	page 49
Slowing Down My Reflexes	page 52
Luck and Its Effect On Self Defense and Creation of Martial Arts Styles	page 54
1980 Creation of Techniques Based On the Spirit of the Individual Animal	page 56
Bellevue Kung-Fu Club	page 58
No Cheers For the big Chinese Guy	page 64
The 1980s	page 66
Saving a Life	page 72
The Next Two Greatest Influences of My Life	page 74
Enlightenment of the "Why" of Taking Martial Arts	page 75
Acceptance By Canadian Sifus	page 76
Acceptance By Seattle Sifus	page 77
1988 Yee Jong Kune Do Transition Into Yee Jong Pai	page 77
Semi-retired in 1989	page 78
The 1990s	page 78

First Instructional DVD	page 82
The New Millennium	page 82
Public Recreation	page 84
The Difference Between Sport and Actual Combat	page 87
Iron Palm Training	page 90
Firearms?	page 91
Masters and Martial Arts Friends	page 93
The World of Martial Arts	page 97
Great clay, or a Great Potter?	page 98
The Kung-Fu Anti-Christ	page 99
Non-Typical Kung-Fu Master	page 99
People I Had Promoted to Sifu Status	page 102
Ranking	page 105
Why I Used the Title of Grandmaster	page 106
Eight Words a Martial Artist Should Live By	page 107
Quality Student / Quality Person	page 107
Bigotry and Prejudice I Have Endured	page 107
Training Family Members	page 110
My Birthday Parties	page 113
The Joy of Teaching	page 115
"Those that can do. Those that can't teach." HOGWASH!!!!	page 117
Teaching Workshops	page 117
The Satisfaction of Appreciation	page 118
Behind Every Great Man There's a Great Woman	page 118
Most Severe Kung-Fu Injury	page 120
Unforeseen Benefits of Kung-Fu	page 121
Grief	page 121
Extended Family	page 123
What We Are Today is the Product of What We've Experienced in the Past	page 124
Could You Have Ever Imagined	page 126
The Future of Yee Jong Pai	page 126
Retired in 2009	page 127
My Journey	page 127

The Beginning

My journey started with my birth in Seattle, Washington in 1956. My parents were both immigrants from China. I was a huge baby, weighing in at 9 pounds 10 ounces. I was 23" long and had a full head of hair. I was a "monster!" My poor little Chinese mother was about 5'3". I remembered she would tell me about how difficult it was to walk with me when I was still in the womb. She used to say that it was very hard to get in the bathtub while carrying me. My father stated since I was born with a full head of hair, the nurses actually combed it.

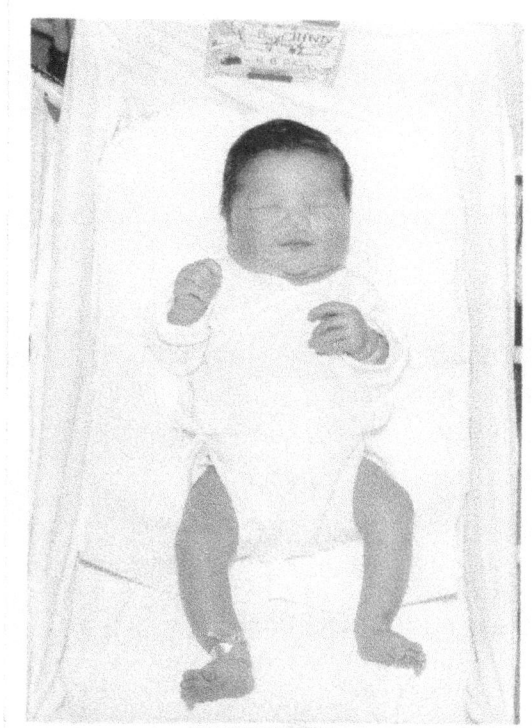

9 lbs 10 oz, 23 inches long and with a full head of hair

I have an older sister, and two younger brothers. My parents were very conservative. So we did everything together when we were young. It was mostly because we had nowhere to go. We weren't allowed very far from the house. My youngest brother Grant was born mentally handicapped. This would affect our family and we would pull together to make things work.

As I was growing up my parents noticed that I was very talkative and not bashful. Mom used to say when I was 4 years old, down at Lake Washington; I would walk right up to strangers and start a conversation. I would make fast friends and then share their bread to feed the ducks. Mom marveled that I was outgoing and not shy.

My father came to this country in 1930, when he was 12 years old.

My mother and my sister Susan came here in 1952.

We spoke the Toisonese dialect, a variant of Cantonese. Some words were very similar, but others were very different. The tones are different as well. This would be a challenge as very few people speak this dialect. It is different enough that the Cantonese-speaking people could not understand us.

The Three Greatest Influences In My Life

When growing up the three greatest influences in my life were my father, my mother, and my sister.

1956 my first Christmas with my father

Father

James H. Chinn was my father. As a young boy my father had learned a little Kung-Fu from an uncle. He immigrated to Seattle, Washington in 1930 by himself. He was only 12 years old at the time and lived in Chinatown with an uncle. He worked as a "Pantry Boy" in a Chinese restaurant. Within a year he moved out with his 14 year old cousin. They both shared an apartment. Years later my father went back to China. As an adult he would train in Choy Li Fut Kung-Fu under Grandmaster Cheong Mo.

My father moved around a little bit having lived in China, Seattle, Alaska, back to China, and finally back to Seattle. He was a marksman at an early age. He told me that as a kid in Seattle, he used to hustle the adults at the shooting gallery, at the Penny Arcade. As an adult he owned a pool hall in Chinatown in the mid-1950s. He later worked a long career at Boeing.

He was always a great shot, and had been an outdoorsman as an adult. He loved fishing and hunting. At age eight he started teaching me both Kung-Fu and target shooting.

I loved hearing my father's numerous stories of Kung-Fu heroes. These stories influenced me quite a bit. His story telling was great and I could feel history being explained to me. The lessons I took from the stories taught honor, righteousness and bravery. I also listened to his many stories of fishing and hunting exploits. I could see in his eyes and smile the pride that my father had in his accomplishments.

As a 14 years old and I took my hunter safety course so I could receive a hunting license and get to go hunting with my father. This was at the Seattle police range 38 years ago. At the conclusion of the class the instructor took all the kids and the parents to the trap range. As a reward, he gave all the kids an opportunity to shoot at a few clay pigeons. We weren't that great at that time. The instructor then asked the parents to try to hit some clay pigeons.

There were two positions that the participants would fire from. My father was on the left. When the kids were shooting most of us missed our clays. So my father decided to load both chambers of the double barrel shotgun just in case the other parent missed. Father held his shotgun at port arms. One of the parents yelled "pull" and the two clay pigeons were up in the air. My father quickly shouldered his shotgun and shot his clay pigeon creating a cloud of dust. The other parent missed and my father quickly locked onto his clay pigeon and shot it too. My father did this two more times, each being double hits.

We headed back to the class area when the shooting was all done. I remember feeling very proud of my father. Even the instructor was very impressed with my father's shooting abilities and chatted with them all the way back to the clubhouse.

I fondly described my father as "Archie Bunker from hell." He was from another era and was very opinionated. He was a teenager in the mid-1930s. When I was a teenager I remember sitting in his chair. Just like Archie Bunker he would say: "Get out of my chair!" He was not racist, but had his opinions on the crookedness of the church, politicians and the police. His bad temper provided the "from hell" part. This coupled with the fact that he was an expert shot and a Kung-Fu master made my father a formidable force that needed to be treated with the utmost respect.

My father's stories of Kung-Fu, fishing and hunting, had a huge effect on me. These stories inspired me to study them as subjects. Wanting to excel, I read everything I could on the subjects. It was largely because of my father's inspiration that I became a Kung-Fu expert, shot competitively, and enjoyed working in the outdoor sporting goods, and firearms industry.

My mother carrying me at Christmas 1956

Mother

Sil Fong Chinn was my mother's name. My mother went through many hardships throughout the years. She was challenged by her in-laws, and was not treated well by them. My father spent much time away from home in the early years as a merchant marine, and was here in the United States. After she went through the Japanese occupation in her region of China, she came to the United States in 1952.

I learned from my mother unconditional love, and self-sacrifice. She did everything for us. She worked in the garment industry. Every day after work, she came home to cook dinner for us. How she could find the energy to cook her wonderful dishes, after a long day at work, was amazing.

When I was young she never approved of my martial arts or my hunting and fishing. She thought it was a waste of time. Often she told me that I should be studying schoolwork instead. I remember she used to say that I was supposed to be very smart, because of the shape of my ears.

Through my mother, I learned to worry. If she loved you, she worried about you. I remember all the years when my father went hunting in Yakima. She would stand at the window wondering when he would make it home. It was usually late Sunday night, and in the 60s and 70s there weren't cell phones. Once he made it home, and her stress and worry would go away.

She enjoyed simple pleasures and was never extravagant. Listening to Chinese music tapes, or working on her garden, eventually gave way to watching her Chinese video tapes.

Her passion was always us. She always wanted the best for us.

Even when we were children, she always ate the leftovers, so that we could eat the fresh, better food. Only when we understood what she was doing, did we fight over the leftovers.

She valued others as well. Her friends received only her most perfect pastries, and my brother-in-law Wally always got the big piece of chicken. Her grandchildren always brought a smile to her face. She could always find something positive about each of them.

My mother had a lifetime of self-sacrifice for her family. Always hoping for the best, caring, teaching, nurturing and loving.

Susan

My sister Susan has always been the BEST. She exemplifies goodness, kindness and generosity. She has always looked out and taken care of me. Then again she is such a wonderful person who takes care of everyone in the family that needed support and help.

Hyesim, my second ex-wife, once stated that she had never seen a brother and sister as close as Susan and me. She stated that we were like sisters. My first response was "Hey…" but then I thought about it and I understood what she meant.

Susan was nine years older than me. She always thought about taking care of our family. I remember my mother stating that as a child Susan stated that she was going to buy her a coat with a fur collar and a big chair for my father. She fulfilled these gift promises.

Susan carrying a very large Allen Christmas 1956

As a child, she was always trying to help us and give us money for doing chores. We would save up the money and she would help us buy presents for birthdays, Christmas, Mother's Day and Father's Day. Growing up I always received the best presents from her.

When I was about seven, or eight years old and I was in love with dinosaurs and reptiles. I remember saving up money for mail order chameleons. Today's reptiles were decedents of the dinosaurs of the past. I thought that when I grew up, maybe I could be a paleontologist. One day Susan stated: "Someday, you'll forget all about dinosaurs and lizards, and you'll discover girls." I disagreed with her and I made a two dollar bet with her. I was certain that I would never give up my dinosaurs and reptiles. She was right and I lost! I have yet to pay this bet off.

Funny we had our tonsils out at the same time. I was about eight years old and she was 17. We shared the same hospital room. It was reassuring with my big sister there. About eight years later, we also got our braces at the same time. Together we drove over to Dr. Von Zanner in Mercer Island, for our work.

1974 hammock fun with my sister Susan

One day I excitedly told my sister that I had discovered what I wanted to be when I grew up! I was a sophomore in high school and had taken an accounting class. I was doing great and accounting's checks and balances held my attention like a game. So I told my sister that I wanted to be an accountant when I grew up. She stated: "I can't see you sitting behind a desk all day working with numbers." I thought about it and she was right. I immediately lost interest in accounting (my A.D.D. kicked in). At the end of the trimester the teacher offered to give a half credit of A, or a full credit of C. I choose to take the full credit of C.

As a teenager, Susan and I always did errands together. She was always generous and even helped me buy my suit for my prom. I remember I took her to a popular clothing store for young men, when looking for the suit. I found what looked great in my eyes, but she stated that the material wasn't very good, and almost see through. She took me to Bon Marche and found a suit with good quality, style and was at a good price.

I was happy for my sister on her wedding day, but I started to get sad. I started missing her, even though she was in front of me in her wedding gown. My eyes started to tear up, because I felt I was losing my sister. My brother-in-law's younger brother Ron was filming my tears on Super 8 film. I was starting to get a little upset, but Ron stated he wasn't making fun of me; he was just filming the moment.

We always found things to do together. After marriage we would still find the time to hang out. Family was always important to us. We would go on family vacations, and we still hang out to this day.

Susan was an investment genius. She saved and invested to ensure her family was always financially strong. This fell in perfect alignment with her generous, caring nature.

*

I cannot conclude these thoughts on Susan, without commenting on my brother-in-law Wally Lee. He is truly the best guy in the world. I am very glad my precious sister married this perfect match. I know most brother-in-laws don't usually give such praise, but he is an amazing human being. Selfless, generous, caring, thoughtful and kind, he is the perfect partner for my sister.

Susan and Wally

My mother used to say that Wally was one in a million. There are no other son-in-laws that take care of their in-laws like Wally did. He helped talking care of my aging parents when their health was failing and did so with much love, and concern. He truly is the best!

These are the biggest influences in shaping who I am today.

How I Started In Kung-Fu

When I was eight years old I wanted to take Karate classes. In the early 1960s television shows like The Detectives, 77 Sunset Strip, and Surfside 6. I was impressed with the power of the "Karate Chop" and the knee strike. Since these shows identified the ancient, secret art as Karate, I wanted to learn it.

Back then, Hollywood knew very little about martial arts. The knee strike and knife hand were the only techniques I saw in the mid 60s. Far from what we see today, there were no flashy kicks, joint locks and throws. Certainly there was no such thing as "wire work" back then. Still, even with the most basic of techniques demonstrated on the television, I was "hooked." I felt that with learning Karate, I could have power, and toughness.

One day I asked my father if I could have some money to take Karate lessons. He asked: "Why do you want to take Karate?" I replied: "For self defense and exercise!" Dad looked me in the eye and asked if that was the real reason. I affirmed my interest. Dad then said: "I'm going to teach you something better than Karate. I'm going to teach you Kung-Fu. It is what all martial arts come from."

I looked him in the eye and I asked: "Dad, are you making this up?" He laughed and assured me this was real.

I didn't know that my father was a Choy Li Fut Kung-Fu master. My father was just my father. This was the same man who lied to me a year earlier. I remembered we were at the Cedar River getting river rocks for my mother's friend. My father caught a small 4" trout that legally had to be thrown back in. I saw the little fish and like any little kid asked: "Can I keep it?" My father stated: "Okay, but I'm going to put it back in the river now, and I'll catch it back before we leave." And I replied: "Okay."

How can I trust him with this story in mind? Besides, I never heard of Kung-Fu. I was an eight year old and eight year olds know everything.

*

My brother Steven and I used to tussle all the time. You know… typical for two brothers. I was 15 months older and even as a seven, or eight year old, I was creating wrestling moves. I always won and my father would hear about the conflicts from our mother when he was home.

My father worked swing and graveyard shifts at Boeing, so it was tough to catch him with any free time during the week. Weekends were also a challenge, as was always hunting, or fishing whenever he had the chance.

My father stated that he would teach Steven Kung-Fu so my brother would eventually kick my butt! So, my father started to teach him, and I would stand around begging to learn. He continually refused, but one day he finally broke down said: "Okay." I was finally able to learn Kung-Fu. We always had horse stance training. He also made us do push-ups. Eventually, we started to do basic blocks. That led to basic strikes and a kick. As we got more involved, I quickly learned and became better than Steven. He got discouraged and then quit.

I continued training under dad. His many stories about Kung-Fu heroes kept my interest in learning Kung-Fu.

Training Under My Father and Alone

Training under dad was a double-edged sword. On the one hand I was learning Chinese Kung-Fu and I knew that I would be empowered by learning this art. On the other hand, training was very slow and very boring after a while. I had A.D.D. and so the very traditional classical training methods didn't keep my interests for very long. My attention would be held by learning new techniques or applications, but once I started to do the repetitious training to ensure good fundamentals, my little mind was bored and all over the place.

My father was a traditionalist. So fundamentals were everything. Developing a very good horse stance was a foundation for everything. Sitting at a horse stance was very boring and I was easily distracted. I remember when my father was not watching I would cheat and get out of the horse stance to rest my legs. I would then quickly sit back in the horse stance when I heard him coming back into the room.

As an eight-year-old I was bright and could grasp much of what my father wanted to teach. Unfortunately, he worked swing shift in graveyard for Boeing. So when he was at home I was usually at school. My father's weekends were taken up by his hobbies of fishing and hunting, or of the numerous home projects he was always building and working on. So finding the time to learn from my father was a challenge in itself.

1966 Sifu James H. Chinn performing outstanding Choy Li Fut techniques

Horse stance training was important as well as other stances. From there we learned basic blocks. Finally we learned a strike or two and a couple kicks. Training was very slow and sporadic because of my father's schedules.

*

About 1966 my father was teaching Kung-Fu to a coworker. He was a very large Black gentleman named Skinner. He and my father were used to calling each other by his last names so it was the first time I heard my father called Chinn. Skinner was over at our house and learned privately from my father. There I would watch him try to learn forms.

My father stated that Skinner was amazingly strong. At Boeing were they both worked, Skinner had reportedly moved a machine weighing 500 pounds by himself. Skinner would religiously come in train with dad and I would watch. Eventually my father thought that Skinner should train in another Chinese martial art to accomplish his ultimate goal. So my father recommended Skinner to take up Tai Chi.

Skinner eventually found a suitable Tai Chi instructor. Skinner was so dedicated that every other week he would drive up to Vancouver B.C. to train under this Tai Chi master. Skinner would occasionally still come to visit my father. It was on one of his visits that he gave me my first martial arts book. It was a book on Shaolin Kung-Fu written by Robert W. Smith.

1966 Sifu James H. Chinn Choy Li Fut Staff Techniques

As a fifth grader this was my prized possession. I remember taking it to school to show my friends, because none of them knew that there was anything like Kung-Fu. So like many foolish elementary aged kids, I left my prized book in my desk. And after coming back from lunch my prized book was missing. I felt a great loss, and understood that sometimes you can't trust anyone.

*

Seeing written material about the martial arts with the photos for how movements should progress, gave me an interest in reading up more about various martial arts styles and cultures. At this early age I had already figured out that I should try to understand other styles and techniques that I might encounter, in order to defeat those different styles and techniques.

I think back to when I was about 13 years old. I was just learning about Chinese weaponry from my father. We didn't have any practice weapons back then, so he would use mop sticks for staffs, a machete for a saber, and a chain for a steel whip. My father also drew pictures of the various weapons he was familiar with.

Excited, I kept asking him which one was "the best" weapon. I asked if the spear was good. He said yes. I asked if the straight sword was good, I heard yes again. What about the three section staff? "Yes!" he replied. I was a little confused. He stated that they were all good. "So, which one is the best?" I asked. Tired of my questioning, my father stated: "If you're good, you're good." I didn't truly "get it," but I knew better than continue my series of questions.

A few years later, I finally understood what my father was trying to say. He was trying to say that all the weapons were good. It was the person wielding them who actually made the difference.

My father was telling me about a duel he had witnessed when he was a young boy. Two masters were selling herbs too close to each other on the same street. Kung-Fu masters selling herbal medicine was a common occurrence in old China. Feeling the new master had infringed on his territory, the first master took offense to it. Both masters and their students began to argue. Things were stated without diplomacy and soon the masters had started a duel to the death. The first master brought out his double butterfly knives. These weapons were thick, but like short double sabers. The new master brought out his tiger fork, a large, long trident for fighting tigers.

Both masters performed several guarded attacks, trying to feel each other out. This was a game with serious and final consequences. They were careful not to make a deadly mistake. Finally, the first master had opened his stance and guard. The new master felt he could take advantage of this opening. My father then asked: "Which one do you think won?" I quickly replied: "The master with the tiger fork!"

My father smiled and slowly shook his head. He stated that the first master with the double butterfly knives had opened his stance and guard to entice the new master for an attack. The new master wanted to make short work of it and went straight in for a death strike to the chest. As the tiger forks tips raced towards the first master, the two smaller bladed weapons caught and trapped the large tiger fork head.

The new master knew he had made the ultimate mistake and was going to pay for it with his life. He apologized and begged for forgiveness. The first master released the tiger fork and accepted the apology. The new master then gave the first master a monetary tribute for selling on the first master's street and left the city.

I was totally surprised, how could these two much smaller weapons defeat the larger, powerful tiger fork. I then understood what my father had stated previously: "If you're good, you're good." It was the skill and the man behind the weapon that mattered most.

*

As a teenager I started to look at martial arts magazines with fascination. In my early teens only Black Belt and Karate Illustrated were available. I remember reading about martial artists like Bruce Lee and Chuck Norris in the late 60s. I seemed to have a talent for looking at the pictures and being able to piece together how movements were to be made. Reading about the different styles and martial artists gave me new fuel for my desire to learn more.

*

I found out about Dim Mak during some of my research. I asked my father if there actually was such a thing as the "death touch." He assured me that there was such a technique. He stated that Dim Mak could kill instantly, or there could be a delay in death that could last weeks, or months. Some techniques could also cause paralysis. I was ecstatic to find out that there was indeed such a powerful technique.

I asked my father if he knew Dim Mak. My father then stated that a master in Dim Mak would be the kind of person, that if someone came up to him and spit in his face, the master would thank him and walk away. He stated: "I couldn't learn Dim Mak because I have a bad temper."

At that point I understood that with ultimate power, comes the greatest responsibility. To possess the knowledge and ability to cause death must be tempered by the power to control oneself not to use it.

*

In my early teens my father purchased a double straight sword made of wood for me. Previously he had taught me basic saber. My father was amazed how fast I was learning the movements of a double straight sword. He taught me the double-figure eight, and I was able to learn that within a few minutes.

I continued to train and practice on my own. I was still reading about various martial arts styles and whenever I could see pictures, I would be able to translate the movements in the pictures to movements that I could actually do.

I also had friends in different Kung-Fu styles, as well as Karate and Judo. Working out and watching my friends, I started to pick up and understand some of their techniques. This slowly added to my bank of martial arts techniques.

My father called my style "dap thuey" Kung-Fu. "Dap thuey is the Toisonese pronunciation of the Americanized Chinese words "chop suey." He meant to say that all my techniques were bits and pieces put together, similar to the popular Americanized Chinese dish. In the early 1970s my father was not impressed with the combination style I was creating.

At one point I was training three to four hours a day. I strongly desired to be proficient in various Kung-Fu movements and only large amounts of practice would help those techniques to become polished. My knowledge was fairly limited at that time, so what techniques I knew had to be exceptional to be truly effective.

In the early 1970s, a new martial arts magazine came to the scene. Inside Kung-Fu was a fresh new look and gave new information about the little reported Chinese martial arts. Black belt and Karate Illustrated usually reported on Japanese and Korean martial arts. On rare occasions those magazines might have a small article on some Chinese martial artists or style. So the introduction of Inside Kung Fu was truly amazing.

Only in the 1980s did my father find positive things to say about the style I had created. No longer did he refer to my style as "dap thuey" Kung-Fu. He was proud of me for what I had developed and the skills that I possessed. His approval meant very much to me.

Growing Up

I was a typical kid growing up, except that I was a second generation Chinese. I spoke Toisonese when I was home with my mother and usually used English when speaking to my father. In school I was a typical American kid. Everyone was trying to get good grades and hanging out with friends. At home I would be an obedient son and follow Chinese customs. Growing up I would get used to Chinese holidays and the rituals that go with them.

New Year's (Chinese, or American) was full of customs that we had to follow. We couldn't answer the phone, open mail, or turn on the radio, or watch television. Since this was a very important day, you would not want bad news to start off your new year. Bad news would be a bad omen. On this day, we could not wash our hair, or sweep the floor. We ate specific foods for the day and the traditional dishes had special meanings. All in all, everything was to have a good start and good luck for the upcoming year.

1960 me, Grant and Steven

April 1961 at Seward Park

I remember a time when my mother wanted my brother Steven and I to work on our handwriting. I was about eight years old at the time. It was the summer and we were supposed to write several pages each day to develop good hand writing. I just discovered carbon paper. My sister had some for her schoolwork; she was nine years older than me. So, I made copies of my handwriting with the carbon paper. At first my mother was fooled, but she soon figured it out.

We were about to get the yu-han. It was the traditional Chinese parents' weapon of choice. It was the bamboo feather duster. Usually made with a bamboo stick, half of it was covered with chicken feathers. Holding the wood part and you dust furniture, figurines, vases and other items. Holding the feather part, parents "dust" children needing punishment.

1960 Allen, Richard, Grant and Steven

1960 kids at Volunteer Park

My mother was busy for a moment, so Steven and I went to our room. As the older brother by 15 months, I came out with a "bright idea." I suggested we should wrap our legs with newspaper. We did so and put back our jeans to cover the newspapers. We walked over to our mother and she struck us a couple of times with the yu-han. We pretended each of the hits hurt us and after receiving our punishment, were sent to our room.

1960 Asian American family in Seattle

Once we went to our room, we closed the door and we couldn't help laughing. My mother over heard us laughing, and wondered why the boys were laughing since they were just punished. She opened the door and saw us with our pants down and our legs wrapped in newspaper. We removed the newspaper and received our punishment without the paper armor.

Note this was the 1960s and this was not considered child abuse. This was just discipline.

April 1961

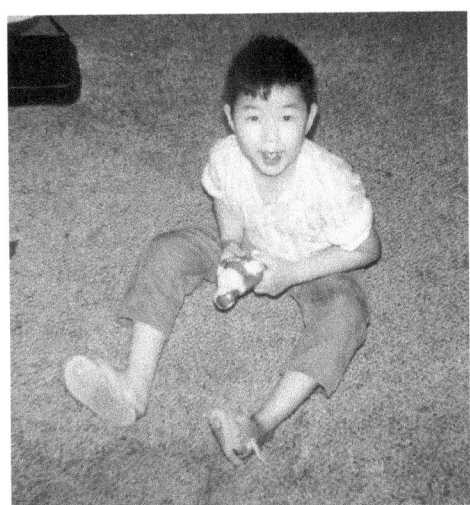
April 1961

December 1961   **July 1962**

1962 with Lulu and her puppy   **1964 with Santa**

I went to Beacon Hill Elementary. I remember Mrs. Smith gave me my 5th grade report card. I believe my grades were: A Art, B Science, C Math, C Language Arts, D Spelling, and E Hand Writing. I hit every letter grade possible. I remember receiving the yu-han with a couple of hits in my outstretched hand from my father.

My 6th grade year at Beacon Hill Elementary started out poorly. I was in Ms. Mock's class and my inability to focus (years later identified as A.D.D.) was evident. I believe I ended up with a couple of D's and the remainder was C's. My parents were not happy with my grades. We moved to South Beacon Hill and my new school was Van Asselt Elementary. They placed me in Mr. Cardin's class. This class was one of two classes that were set up for under achievers. My poor fall trimester grades, made me a good candidate for this class.

The class seemed filled with kids that were destined to become either priests, or murderers. I liked these guys! After a short time, Mr. Cardin came to me and told me my tests and grades from his class were too high, and that I would need to be transferred to another class. I stated that I didn't want to be transferred and preferred to remain in his class. Mr. Cardin said that I could do this, but I could not receive any grade higher than a C. I replied, "Okay," as I really wanted to stay in his class. Luckily I got to remain there.

I believe this class was very good for me. I did well and was able to focus. It helped me to "stabilize" and was positive for my self-esteem.

1966 Christmas

*

One day our family was downtown shopping at Bon Marche. I was 11 ½ years old. I said something (I don't remember what) but it angered my father. I received a five finger dot on top of my head. It did hurt and I remember tears rolling down my face as we were going up the escalator. I remembered a similar story he told us once, about a time when he was in China. A neighborhood kid was being disrespectful and he received a five finger dot on top of his head. He had a shaved head and five swollen bruises appeared on his head. I guess I was lucky. I had hair and no bumps, or bruises.

*

My father spent much of his free time fishing and hunting, but my mother never permitted us to be out there on the lakes, or in the field with him. I was 14 years old and wanted to sneak out to go fishing with my father one Sunday morning. He and I had made plans, so I woke up early and crept out from my basement bedroom. I had placed a couple of pillows under my blanket and locked my door. Quietly, I left through the garage, and met my father outside.

We had a nice morning of fishing and came back home in the early afternoon. When we got back we received a tongue lashing from my mother. She was very upset with us. She stated that she had come downstairs to wake me up for lunch, but I didn't respond. She was worried that something happened to me as I was under the blanket, but didn't respond to her yelling and trying to wake me up. She was almost scared to death. After several frantic attempts to wake me, she finally figured it out. We were in big trouble!

*

Growing up I was fair in basketball and other conventional sports. But my main physical interest would always be Kung-Fu. Because of my pillow and blanket incident and the fact I was getting older, I was permitted to go fishing and hunting with my father. I was always excited to go on these outdoor excursions. We would drive out to Yakima to hunt the corn fields and sometimes Ellensburg at the beet fields. My father was very close to his cousin, and Uncle Joe (Chinn) was always on his hunting adventures. My father would usually select closer locals to fish. Sometimes it was Green Lake, Lake Washington, Lake Kapowsin, Pine Lake, Doloff Lake, Steel Lake, Cedar River, or the Green River.

I remember my father being so tenacious about his hunting and fishing. One winter he took me to the Green River on the sandbar. It was so cold that every other cast, I would have to breathe on the ice in the guide rings to free up the fishing line. After an hour, or so fishing, the wind had kicked up and my father's eyes had watered up. A few minutes later I looked at him and told him not to move. I brought my hand up to his face and flicked a frozen tear off his cheek. After that he agreed it was too cold to be out there steelhead fishing and we left for the warmth of our home.

*

I remember Sunday afternoons in between hunting and fishing seasons. My father and Uncle Joe would be sitting in the living room, watching the American Sportsman. When they couldn't be out in the lakes and fields, they could still watch this nationally broadcasted program that featured hunting and fishing. My mother would make her famous fried chicken. The aroma of her fried chicken filled the air inside the house, as well as outside. Her special seasonings made the chicken outstanding and she had the heat of the oil just perfect. We all had great Sundays back then.

*

In my Junior year at Cleveland High School, I was selected to be a Yell Leader (male cheerleader) for my senior year. The cheerleaders (female) had a separate initiation from ours. Our initiation was very crazy. We met the outgoing Yell Leaders and they dressed us up. We had white t-shirts on and converse high tops. They tied our hands behind our backs, and blindfolded us. They put red panty hose on me, as well as a long, pleated red and white cheerleader's skirt from the 1960s. Some of us had a pair of large balloons inserted under their t-shirts.

The old Yell Leaders took us down to 2nd and Occidental, and had us stand in front of one of the bars. There they made us sing a horrible, embarrassing song. One passerby commented that one of our guys was "cute." After this ordeal they had us walking back to the car. The old Yell Leaders lost track of Gary Uyeji and he ended up walking into a street light pole. That left a mark!

We were then taken to Southcenter Mall. We were walking and then jogging across the parking lot. The old Yell Leader who had me by the arm, said "curb" about a second before I tripped on it. I slammed my knee into the sidewalk. My panty hose was ripped and my knee was bleeding. They took us and put us in front of some shops. This is where they made us do our routine "Two Bits." We were still blindfolded and our hands were still tied up. All we could do was waddle through the routine. Our voices were not very enthusiastic. Southcenter Mall security did not like us, as we were disruptive, so they demanded that we leave.

The old Yell Leaders then took us to Lake Washington for the final phase of the initiation. We were afraid that we were going to thrown in the lake. Instead one by one, they took us to the end of the pier. They had us get down on our hands and knees and congratulated us on becoming official Yell Leaders. We were then slapped on the left and right sides of our head with raw eggs. Then we were struck in the face with a banana cream pie. The upward impact with the banana cream pie was jolting. The old Yell Leaders didn't defrost them early enough and I almost lost a tooth! Surviving the frozen banana cream pie, we were finally official Yell Leaders for the class of 1974.

That following year, we had our sweaters and to complete the rest of our uniform, we chose white cuffed slacks and then purchased red platform shoes from Stanley's Shoes. I was getting very good in my Kung-Fu and had coordination, flexibility, strength and speed. I was young and did things I was lucky not to have received injuries from. I remember I could do a toe touch jump. I foolishly did this in my three inch platform shoes. I was also able to do the Cheerleader's elbow to heel touch. Silly me also would do Kung-Fu jump and flying kicks too.

*

I ended up as a B student throughout high school years. I started attending the University of Washington, but my focus was again misdirected. My grades were not that great. I spent all my time with my girlfriend Cindy. We studied together, had dinner together, we were always together. One evening I was with Cindy at her mother's house in the Rainier Valley. My brother Steven dropped by to visit with us for a bit. When he tried to leave, his old Plymouth would not start. He came back to the house and asked if I could help him push the Plymouth so he could compression start it. I said yes, and was out there pushing his car backwards down the street.

I was half way down the hill, when his car was about another 70 feet away from me. It finally compression started and I turned around walking back to Cindy. She was at the top of the hill. My brother drove up the hill and pulled next to me. He stated: "Do you want a ride?" I said: "Sure." He then told me to get on his hood. I hesitated, as this didn't sound very safe. Then I thought it would be cool to sit on the hood and go up to Cindy and coolly say: "Hi baby." So I told Steven: "Only if you go slow." Steven's voice is fairly low, and I thought I heard him say: "Yeah." He actually said: "Huh?" This was significant.

I got on the hood and Steven started to drive up the hill slowly. As we got near the top, he started going fast. We were probably going 30 miles per hour. We whizzed by Cindy, still going North on the street. She started running after the car. I could hear a pulsating sound as we speed by the parked cars. I was screaming "Stooooooop!" the whole time. Finally Steven slowed down and I flew off the hood. I slid about three, or four feet on the street. My stainless steel Seiko that Susan and Wally bought for me had cut my wrist. The watchband broke and it and the watch were out on the street. The Plymouth stopped just a few feet behind me.

I suddenly got up and ran to Cindy's front door. She got there a few seconds after I did. I was hunched over in pain. My right hand was bleeding and I held my left hand cupped underneath it. I didn't want to get blood on the porch, or on the carpet. Cindy's mom was a clean freak. I walked to the kitchen and was bleeding in the sink. I washed the cuts and pealed skin. Cindy brought me lots of gauze and bandages.

All this time Steven was apologizing and felt very bad. He offered me his car and other items saying he was too dangerous to own them. I told him it was all right. I knew he didn't mean for me to get hurt. I was laying on the sofa in the living room, when Cindy said: "Okay, which hospital are we going to?" I stated I was alright, and all I needed was Tylenol. She insisted we go right away to a hospital so I selected Providence.

Steven drove us and I got treated right away. My injuries included: a severely sprained right ankle, contusion on the right knee, bruised hip, contusion on the stomach, small rocks were imbedded in both palms, contusion on my knuckles, three inches of skin on my right fore finger was damaged, left wrist was cut, contusions on the left wrist, contusion on the right upper chest, and a contusion on my right cheek. With all this "road rash" the medical staff thought I fell off a skateboard.

That night Steven helped me hobble back to our home. It was really late at night, so my parents were already asleep. I stayed in bed and the next morning I stated that I didn't feel so well and stayed home. My hands and wrists were bandaged up so much, that I looked like a mummy in those areas. My right wrist had locked up and was extremely painful to move it. It was very weak too. My sister happened to have the day off and visited me at home. I remember Susan was so sweet she fed me. My father had made ham steaks that afternoon, but in my condition I couldn't hold a knife, or a fork. Susan was a real angel and I really did look pitiful.

My mother saw all my injuries later that afternoon and I made up a story I fell down the Montlake stairs leading to the parking at the University of Washington. My mother told me I shouldn't be so clumsy and I simply replied yes.

Early Equipment

Back when I was training hard as a teenager, we had no real equipment to work with. No uniforms, no striking bags, no weaponry... nothing!

When I learned from my father, it was in regular clothing. The techniques I learned were performed in jeans and t-shirts. My father was teaching me Choy Li Fut Kung-Fu, which was a Southern style. His style did not do too much in the area of kicking, so the street clothing was not too much of a hindrance.

Since I had no equipment to enhance my striking and kicking abilities. I had to be creative. I therefore, constructed improvised striking equipment.

*

I was kicking only waist high with my side kicks. I decided to use a small copper cow bell tied to a length of fishing line. I started with the bell at waist height. As I felt more comfortable and natural kicking, I would shorten the length of the fishing line a couple of inches. I would keep kicking until the new height would become natural. I would then repeat the process over again. I finally was able to kick over six feet high with my side kicks.

*

To develop more power I had to have a striking dummy. I decided to take some of my father's construction supplies and make a makeshift makiwara. I took a rectangular piece of plywood and I cut a matching piece of Masonite. I placed 2" x 4" pieces of wood at the edges and nailed everything together. I then found old rags, and old clothing (I shouldn't have used my father's 1930s suits) wrapped them around the makiwara, and then placed them inside of a couple of burlap sacks.

This striking dummy served me well. It offered enough resistance, and I could hear the makiwara echo sound whenever I punched or kicked it well. It was suspended by a long rope in my parents' carport. I used it in this fashion for about six months. I then cut a couple of holes on the upper section. I placed a mop stick through the holes. This acted as arms. I could practice deflecting, blocking and grabbing, while still punching, or kicking with power.

*

To create speed, I knew that I need a target to focus on but not offer heavy resistance. I had read in one of my books, using a silk scarf could enhance speed. I had an acetate scarf (it was actually my Apache Tie from the 70s) and decided to use it for my speed training. I tied the scarf up in my room and proceeded to train in instantaneous strikes.

My speed increased and I was not telegraphing (slightly moving) so my opponent would have greater difficulty in reacting to my fast strikes. The low impact of the scarf permitted me to focus on speed without resistance.

*

Another item I used to increase my speed was candles. I discovered this in one of my martial arts books and trained to punch out the candle with a fast punch. The air turbulence created by a very fast punch, would blow out the candle flame.

*

In order to train my hands and toughen the various hand weapons, I used a six pound bean bag. I went to the grocery store and purchased what appeared to be hard beans. I then placed them in a few layers of burlap. Sewing it all up, I had my six pound bean bag. I would practice the various hand techniques and toughen my hands, preparing them for impact.

*

I originally didn't have any weapons to train with. Weapons are an important and large part of Kung-Fu. Training without weapons, would be like practicing baseball without a bat. You could do catching and throwing, but you would be missing a big part of the game without the ability to practice with a bat.

My first staff was nothing more than a mop stick. This was eventually replaced with a six foot 1 1/8" oak rod that I purchased from a lumberyard. My training for the saber was done with a heavy Bolo machete. Not quite the same, but it had a large single edged blade and it was somewhat a similar shape to a Chinese saber.

When I started training in the steel whip, I created a simple version with steel chain, an eye bolt, oak for a handle and I made a torpedo tip out of stainless steel on a grinder. This steel whip was crude, but functional. I did learn the very difficult poking technique with this improvised steel whip.

I even made throwing stars out of sheet metal. I drew a pattern on sheet metal and used sheet metal shears to cut and create the throwing stars.

*

My favorite training apparatus that I created was called Norman Numb Nuts. I made this unit in 1980 and soon it earned its name. I worked at Auburn Sports and Marine and they had large boat bumpers (fenders). I used two of the 20 inch bumpers. They were tough, durable and could take a beating. I tied the two together and then tied a long piece of rope from the ceiling to the top eyelet of the top boat bumper.

This unit would dance, sway, bob and weave and was difficult to hit. At times the bottom boat bumper would kick upward or even thrust forward. One day one of my students decided to punch Norman hard. When the heavy impact landed, the bottom boat bumper kicked upward, striking him sharply in the groin. From that day on it was known as Norman Numb Nuts.

First Uniforms

In 1973 my sister Susan made my first actual Kung-Fu uniform. We didn't have any idea what it should really look like. My mother stated that the pants were similar to pajamas. Susan and I found a pattern for a shirt with slightly "balloon" shaped sleeves. She modified the pattern and made the shirt a "pull over" and changed the collar to be very small.

The material selected was satin and it was colored blue and white, as my mother did not want it all black. She was concerned it was funeral colors. She didn't want it all white for the same reason. She also thought black and white might be too similar to funeral colors also, so the only way we could go was royal blue and white. My sister got on the sewing machine and sewed away. This was my first Kung-Fu uniform.

The following year my mother decided she would make me another uniform. This time she lightened up on the color scheme and decided it was acceptable to have a black and white uniform. My mother chose a heavier duty satin material. She was truly amazing. She made the jacket without a pattern. She did the "Chinese" collar and "frog" buttons from memory. I remember watching her make the "frog" buttons and was amazed how she cut the satin into small pieces and then tie them up into the ball type knot using a small hook.

After graduating high school, I decided to dye the first uniform black. What my mother didn't know wouldn't hurt her (or me). So I purchased some Rite black dye and boiled and stirred away. Somehow, the black dye turned the royal blue and white satin into navy blue. I guessed it would be fine, as I wouldn't get in trouble if my mother saw me in it.

ADD/ADHD

As a child growing up, I was always very active, too active in fact. My mother nicknamed me "sang malai." This was Toisonese for "Wild Monkey." I was always all over the place. It was always difficult to stay on task and in one place. However, I always had lots of energy and tasks that did keep my attention were always completed in record time.

My mind would move fast, and if I was in a situation that moved too slowly, I would get bored easily and my mind would wander. If there was something that could actually keep me interested, I could concentrate on it and more important, stick with it.

In school I had minor issues leading to 6th grade, but they seemed to stabilize after my transfer to Van Asselt Elementary. The continued interests I had were instilled to me by my father. Anything related to Kung-Fu, hunting and fishing were the only things that kept my attention. I excelled in my knowledge of these subjects.

My knowledge in these areas gave me the opportunity to get jobs in teaching martial arts, selling outdoor sporting goods, and competing in martial arts tournaments, trap shooting and combat pistol shooting.

However, it wasn't until about 1985 that I learned and understood Attention Deficit Disorder and Attention Deficit Hyperactivity Disorder. Our five year old son Jason was diagnosed by the Kent School District Psychologist to have behavior issues and would need counseling. My wife and I decided to take a class about ADD at Group Health Cooperative. The class started by Dr. Connie McDonald (head of OB at the time) and a nurse, each stating that they were ADD kids. They each described her challenges as children. They stated that because of a difference in biochemistry, the brain receives information differently than from people without this condition. They told us that at about 15, 16 years of age, the individual would learn how to cope with these issues. They did state that this is a lifelong condition. It can never go away. We must learn how to cope with it.

This class was invaluable and we discovered that few people, including teachers and school district psychologists, understood what ADD/ADHD was. They didn't know much, if anything about this condition and did not have a clue on accommodations and support needed to help the students.

This gave me insight on my own history. I discovered that I had the same symptoms! Everything discussed in the class seemed to apply to me. While I was able to use the information to help my sons, Jason and Brandon, I was also able to better understand my own ADD/ADHD.

Childhood Heroes

When I was little, Superman was my hero. He had powers only we could dream of. The ability to fly, x-ray vision, heat vision, super speed, super breath, and invulnerability, were just too exciting to think about. I remember my mother making "Superman" capes when I was about five years old. My brother and I used crayons to mark a big "S" on them. We would run around the house and pretend we were flying. We bounce on available beds and pretend we were flying. One day we were bouncing on our living room sofa. Steven took a bad bounce and landed, hitting his head. He ended up with an eye injury and had to wear glasses. That is how "Superman" helped give him glasses.

*

I liked special shaped bandages that were available in 1961. I put them all over my arms as if they were tattoos. Susan seeing a big waste put a remaining box of these bandages up high in a corner cabinet in our kitchen. I remember looking at that box, way high up in the corner. I wanted them. So I was determined to get them. It was so high up there, but I had thoughts on how to get up there. My mother was at the kitchen table, concentrating on writing a letter to relatives in China. She didn't notice me pushing the baby feeding table to the corner.

The baby feeding table had caster wheels and was easy to move to the corner. It was also very silent. Next there was a small green step that needed to be moved to the baby feeding table. I quietly moved that to the top of the table. I then climbed onto the top of the baby feeding table. Then I climbed the small step stool and was finally able to reach the animal shaped bandages.

I grabbed the metal box and just I did so, the step stool/baby feeding table combination started moving. My little 5 year old mind raced and remembered Superman burrowing through the ground. Somehow with equally quick movements, I placed the metal box of bandages under my left arm and started to fall. Going head first to the floor, I stuck out my arm as I had seen Superman do.

My little arm broke as it hit the floor. Bad for the arm, but at least I didn't break my neck! My mother rushed to me and moved my arm asking if it hurt. I cried louder when the arm moved. Once she was certain it was bad, she called my father at work. Dad rushed out from his swing shift at Boeing. I remember him taking me to the hospital. I thought it was odd that I broke my arm, but they put me in a wheel chair.

I ended up getting a cast, and because the break was a certain way, they angle of the cast was horrid. I remember my right hand almost touched my left collarbone. I was wheeled back out and my father took me home. This is how Superman helped me save my neck, but broke my arm.

*

My father loved watching Westerns. So with one television in the house, I got to see quite a few Westerns. John Wayne became one of my heroes. I liked what seemed to be his philosophy: respect me and I'll respect you, hit me and I'll hit you back. He always seemed to stand for what was right. He always played the good, moral hero. He always won.

*

In the 60s, Bruce Lee entered my young life. He played Kato in the Green Hornet. My friends and I thought he was great!!! He could fight like no other and he had those amazing darts that he could throw with great accuracy.

In 1971, I saw him again in ABC's Longstreet. He played the personal martial arts instructor for the blinded attorney. I loved seeing him kick James Franciscus while he was holding an air shield. James Franciscus looked like he was shot from a cannon. In short glimpses, he would give his philosophical view on techniques on the show.

Then his movies hit. First it was Fist of Fury. Everybody rushed to see his movies. As each new film was released, we all went to the theaters to see what he was going to do next. Bruce Lee was the first Asian "superstar!" We never had one before him. Here was a Chinese guy that stood for good, and could kick ass!!! It appeared that the whole world believed that he was a real life superhero.

Until his untimely death in 1973, he influenced many people through his movies. I read whatever I could on him. The biographies were good and explained his life and his actions. It was not until after his death that Ohara Publications published books regarding his fighting methods and his fighting philosophy. The Tao of Jeet Kune Do came out in 1975. Bruce Lee's Fighting Methods came out in 1978. These books gave a different insight on his thinking and philosophy towards the martial arts.

*

When I was young my father was my hero, second only to Superman. After I found that he knew Kung-Fu, I had this parent that was skillful in martial arts, fishing, and hunting. I didn't really have any idea what these activities entailed, but I knew he was good at them. It wasn't until my teen years that I started to understand precisely how good he was at these hobbies.

As I got older I noticed that he was good at carpentry, plumbing, and other things that I had taken for granted. He was "Mr. Fix It" and it seemed that if he didn't know how to repair, or make it, he learned how to do it. My father was quite talented in many areas.

Wanting to Become a Kung-Fu Instructor

As a child I wanted to learn Kung-Fu, and I certainly became very good at it. This interest eventually grew into a desire to someday become an instructor.

Even as an 11 year old, I was taught my friends. I remember I was teaching my friend Michael Baker while I was a 6th grader at Van Asselt Elementary. I continued to train and improve. When I got to Asa Mercer Junior High, I was teaching my friends Ricky Marino and Mike Petta.

At Asa Mercer Junior High and at Cleveland High School, I had written that one of my future occupations could be Kung-Fu Instructor.

The 1970s and the Kung-Fu Craze

With David Carradine and the Kung-Fu television series, the Kung-Fu craze of the 70s took off. There was thirst for Kung-Fu anything, but so many people didn't know what it was, or who was any good. That time period had many unscrupulous individuals claimed to know the different forms of Kung-Fu, but actually knew nothing. Scam artists came out of the woodwork, but so did many talented practitioners.

I was an 8th grader at Asa Mercer Junior High. Once my history teacher found out that I knew Kung-Fu, he had me do a presentation and demonstration. Word got around with the teachers and I ended up doing six or seven such demonstrations. Somehow I ended up in an English class doing a demonstration. Teachers as well as the students wanted to see what Kung-Fu was.

I spoke about the history of Kung-Fu and its influence on other styles of martial arts. I stated that Northern Chinese Kung-Fu styles influenced the kicking styles of Korea, and the Southern Chinese Kung-Fu styles influenced the Okinawan martial arts. I also demonstrated striking, kicking and weaponry. Then one of my acquaintances asked if I wanted to "play Kung-Fu?" My mind was racing as I didn't quite know what he meant. Did he want to "play" spar, "play" fight, or "play" goof around? I figured he wanted to "play" spar, but my father had warned me before, not to spar with people you really don't know of their intention. I felt a little reluctant, as I really did not know his intentions.

So, this person sat in a very high cat stance, and with opposite lead hand and foot. Generally, proper cat stances have the same hand and foot for the lead. Weight distribution is approximately 75% back and 25% front leg. I knew that this was not a very good stance, as he also leaned too much backwards at the waist. I chose to use a side guard (bow and arrow) stance that I had just created. I created the side guard stance to permit quicker side movement.

Neither one of us moved, but another student in the class yelled: "Somebody do something!" So I initiated a medium speed barrage of punches to his mid-section. He blocked the four or five punches, but then did a dishonorable act. He used a claw hand and tried to rake my face. I instinctively moved my head, but felt his finger tips going down my face. Without thinking I immediately launched a 10 finger strike to his mid-section. He flew four feet back and bounced off the classroom door.

He immediately went back to his awkward, high cat stance and I went back to my side guard. This time he charged me with a double hammer fist attack. I quickly moved from the side bow and arrow stance into a cat stance and quickly shot out my right palm. My opponent with his aggressive charge ran his head into my extended palm. This violent impact rocked his world and I asked if we were done. He was groggy and said: "Yes." Word got around and many people found out that I knew Kung-Fu.

*

From David Carradine, people started to migrate to Bruce Lee. What a change! He was someone who really knew what he was doing and learned Kung-Fu for practical, real world use. I remember people started to copy some of his mannerisms. One friend started to eat lunch like Bruce Lee did in Chinese Connection. I remember a scene where he was eating what looked like a barbecued monkey. His chewing was exaggerated, and powerful. It was very funny to see someone eat lunch at the high school cafeteria that way!

*

One day in gym class at Cleveland High School, the gym teacher had us playing line soccer. It was my sophomore year. With both ends of the gym filled with students, the gym teacher would call out three students from each side to attack the soccer ball and attempt to score. All the students at the end lines would try to catch the soccer ball and keep the other team from scoring.

I was up with two of my teammates. The gym teacher would toss, or throw the soccer ball randomly and we would have to rush after it to get control of it. The soccer ball was thrown at the floor and took a high bounce. As it was falling to about seven feet I threw out a high diagonal roundhouse kick. To my shock, just as my foot was nearing the soccer ball, a teammate jumped up trying to "head" the ball.

As his body started to come down, my black and white Converse high tops struck him in the jaw, snapping his head upward. He was still in the air. As he landed on the gym floor he crumpled like a wet noodle. Everyone rushed to see if he was okay. The gym teacher tried to wake him up. Blood was coming out of his mouth. My heart was racing as I thought I had killed him.

He was unconscious for about 10 seconds, but finally started to move. Another student and I helped him to the nurse's office. I felt so bad and kept apologizing. The nurse found that there was a cut in his mouth and that is where the blood was coming from.

He would have to stay there for observation. As I left to go back to class, he indicated he knew it was an accident and it was all right.

*

I was in the after school Kung-Fu Club. It was lead by a staff counselor. There was a senior in the club that had taken Kung-Fu classes previously. He was big and strong and was on our football team. He figured out that I knew quite a bit of Kung-Fu and kept asking me to teach him. I kept refusing and then he started to mess with me.

One day I was in the hall in front of the metal shop. He and his buddies walked by me, and suddenly he grabbed my arms from behind. Then he told his friends to get me. His friends responded with "You get him yourself." as they walked away. There he was still holding me and his buddies just left him. He gave my arms a light shove and said: "You ain't worth it anyway!" Saving face, he then walked away.

This senior happened to be in my accounting class also. One day he approached me and said he had to ask me something in the back of the class. Once we were in the back of the classroom, he pulled out a rusty old straight razor and said: "What are you going to do now?"

I looked at him, straight in the eyes and stated "I'm going to pull your eyes out." He then said, "I'm going to cut ya." I again responded, "I'm going to pull your eyes out." He then asserted, "You don't get it; I'm going to cut ya." I then stated, "I'm still going to pull your eyes out." He looked at me, folded up the straight edge razor and said, "Man, you're crazy!" He went back to his seat and he never tested me again.

*

I believe in my junior year in high school, there appeared a rather large, red haired bully in our gym class. We had just gone through a wrestling session and because of his size and strength, he was dominant. I was smaller and lighter than him so I never wrestled with him. He would bully random people as we would wait for the gym to open. He would sneak up behind his intended victim and put them in a headlock. This became a fairly common occurrence.

One day he walked behind me and suddenly put me in a headlock. I was bent over at the waist and I immediately shot out my right hand. My fingers tips brushed his groin, as I wanted him to know that he should let go. The bully let go of my neck and stated "Chinn if you did that there would have been a fight!" My friend Mike Petta was standing nearby and was watching this incident unfold. Mike replied, "If he did, there wouldn't be a fight!"

For the next couple of months this bully continued to try putting me in a successful hold, but each time, my hand would find its way to his groin. He finally gave up and ceased to play this cat and mouse game with me.

*

I had a friend named Eddie Mar. He and I were standing the hallway near the metal shop one afternoon. Three bullies walked up behind him, and one grabbed him by his arms. One demanded his lunch money. Then one of them questioned: "What if he knows Kung-Fu?" The bully grabbing him asked: "Do you know Kung-Fu?" Eddie responded with: "Um... what do you think?" The bullies let him go and said: "Forget it!" Eddie didn't know any martial arts, but the question he put into the minds of the bullies was enough to make them leave him alone.

*

In the summer of 1973, I was teaching a Kung-Fu class at the University of Washington's Experimental College. Through prompting of my sister Susan, I went through the process of offering a class. My friends

Gary Uyeji and Larry Oliver trained with me at the class. I was given a room in the General Engineering Building, so for each class there was a great deal of moving of desks.

I was teaching all adults, except for Gary and Larry. One of the students asked what school I was from. I responded: "Cleveland." He then stated that was a nice town. I then corrected him and stated high school and not college. Surprised he asked how old I was. He was shocked to find out I was only 16 years old.

*

With Bruce Lee came the popularity of the nunchaku. Several teenagers started to practice and train themselves on the usage of this weapon. I was one of them. These weapons were nicknamed "numbchucks" as the Japanese pronunciation was probably too difficult for some people to say. In Chinese we called them "ling jeek gwun."

Sometimes my friend Ron Fujimoto and I would do impromptu "air sparring" with them. There was no contact, but we could get dangerously close to each other. We even went to parties spinning our sticks around. Gee, what were we thinking back then!

1973 Lion Dance Team Cleveland High School

I demonstrated at our Multi-Cultural Fair in my junior and senior years. I also went to Holy Names Academy to discuss Asian matters. Our group had various topics. My topic was the relationship between American born Chinese and foreign born Chinese, but the students in the assembly really wanted to ask me questions about Kung-Fu. After a brief explanation of my observations as a Chinese American, where I was a bit nervous, I felt much more comfortable answering all the questions which were centered on Kung-Fu.

How it was different from Karate, where it came from, philosophy, etc.… were some of the questions. One question was: "Does Kung-Fu have belts?" My response, after a slight pause to think was: "The belts in Kung-Fu are used to hold up our pants!" The entire audience including my panel was caught off guard, expecting something serious and maybe a little mystical. Everyone broke into hearty laughter! I actually had the whole auditorium laughing, including the nuns and male staff. This delayed our discussion for about five minutes.

*

I accidentally became a participant at Asian Awareness Week activities at Mercer Island High School. Some faculty staff stated that Chinn was supposed to go there and I thought it was me. When we got there I was surprised to meet Jerry Gould, then a 5th degree black belt in Shorin-Ryu Karate. I also saw Wayne Chinn, our old high school counselor and leader of our Kung-Fu Club two years earlier. It was him that the request was probably for. I was the youngest, as I was only 17 years old.

The three of us demonstrated our techniques and all the students were impressed. The students got to see Shorin-Ryu Karate, Praying Mantis Kung-Fu, and my Classical/Non-Classical Kung-Fu style.

1974 Mercer Island High School Martial Arts Demonstration

*

I had a friend that in the mid 70s knew firsthand of my Kung-Fu skills. We used to work out together and we did spar quite a bit. He knew of my skill with firearms also. So one day he surprisingly asked me a question that could have changed my life forever. He started off by complimenting me on my skills, and how I was exceptionally good. He then stated I should become a hit man, and he could be my driver. I was shocked and he wasn't kidding. I respectfully declined the offer, and the subject never was raised up again.

*

In the mid-70s many martial artists started to copy Bruce Lee moves and you could see people bouncing up and down, before they threw their kicks, or punches. Cat yelling sounds also became common amongst what seemed to be "progressive" martial artists.

Bruce Lee's philosophy of trying to be non-traditional and not being tied up in the "classical mess" sprouted many martial artists to believe that they could be free spirited and act like a free jazz musician. Thus martial artists came up with various martial arts destined to failure, because they did not have true understanding in some form of traditional, or classical art. These people were great athletes, but without a foundation to build on, their road was very difficult.

Bruce Lee was unique, and his philosophy and style worked for him. Anyone else could scratch at the surface but not really do what he could do. He had the combat experience, the physical strength, speed and agility that few have. So what worked for him may not work for everyone. He did go through the classical training of Wing Chun Kung-Fu. His philosophy of learning and striping away excess, or useless techniques, was valid for his realization of what he could do and what he understood.

My philosophy was influenced by Bruce Lee's writings, my father's teachings, and other studies of various Sifus' thoughts. I believed that everyone that came to my classes would have to spar. I felt at that time of my life, sparring would be needed to keep up one's speed and reflexes. I believed in Bruce Lee's thoughts that one could not learn how to swim, unless they got into the water. Thus sparring was of the greatest importance in my early days of teaching.

My belief was that there is a combination of ideas and techniques that are valuable in both camps. Modern techniques and training can be effective, but so can classical techniques opponents seldom see, and don't understand.

So through the 1970s I was that mysterious, black sheep martial artist in Seattle. People heard about me, but I didn't have a school to be found. I was a real martial artist, but elusive. I remember a story about a Kung-Fu teacher who looked sort of like David Carradine and would meet his students at a different park location each time. Finally, it came out this guy didn't know any martial arts and was scamming the students. I didn't want any association to flakes like this.

1974 Cleveland High School Kung-Fu Club

As I was graduating from high school, I was speaking to our Vice Principal, Chris Kato. He was a 5th degree black belt in Judo, and extremely talented. We were discussing martial arts and somehow the subject of me teaching at a community center came up. He stated that he would speak to his friend Bill McIntyre, Senior Supervisor at Jefferson Community Center to see if a Kung-Fu class could be taught there. So Mr. Kato made the arrangements for us to meet and I ended up teaching there June of 1974.

The day of my first class, I was nervous not being sure how many students I had. I also didn't know the makeup of the class. I was looking out the north windows of the Social Room and was looking at the tennis courts. I noticed this young lady from behind, as she was facing the other side of the courts. She wore a scarf on top of her head, and had long pretty hair. She wore very short shorts (it was the 70s), and had beautiful long legs. Then I caught myself and remembered I had a class to teach.

As students started to come in the room, I notice the huge diversity. People with different ethnicities, age groups, and genders were represented. Then I noticed that young lady that was on the tennis court walk in. She and her friend ended up being students at that class. Her name was Cindy Goto and by the end of the summer we were dating.

She was a great student and the love of my life. She supported my martial arts and understood just how good I was. BUT she also knew that I must always remain humble. This was one of the many lessons I learned from her.

1974 encouraging words from Chris Kato

I used to try explaining to everyone that what I was teaching was Gung-Fu, as this was the proper pronunciation. It meant "hard work." It has referred to various skills developed through hard work, but most everyone refers Gung-Fu to Chinese martial arts. People would then ask me what was the difference between Gung-Fu and Kung-Fu. I tried to explain that they were the same thing. I actually didn't understand until a couple of years later. I took Chinese History at the University of Washington. It was there that I learned that "K" would be a "G" sound and "K'" is an actual "K" sound. This was English Romanization.

I finally gave up and started spelling it and calling it Kung-Fu.

*

Nick Eagle was a fellow student at Cleveland High School. We became friends because of his interest in Kung-Fu. He knew a little bit and was always trying to improve. He had great abdominal strength and was always showing that off. He had a 255 pound friend step and stand on his stomach. Nick was probably about 140 pounds. I asked Nick if he could withstand my pushing punch. He thought so.

He braced himself and tightened his abdominal muscles. I then placed a sun fist on his stomach. With great acceleration and instantaneous speed my fist pushed into him. The explosive short distance power movement penetrated and overstressed his stomach muscles. They gave in and there was a solid feeling of his spine, as he was propelled into the wall three feet away. Nick was okay, just shaken up a bit.

1974 cat stance in the uniform my mother hand made

I remember during late June of 1974, he used to come by my parent's house and wake me up. I would still be in my pajamas and he would want to spar. Tired, barely awake, with a cowlick in my hair, I would spar with him.

*

I was teaching my friends privately in my parent's backyard. I remember Ron Fujimoto decided that he was going to spar with my brother Steven. I was monitoring the match and acted as judge. They both squared off, Ron suddenly shot out a fast roundhouse sweep to the back of Steven's knee. Steven's stance was so strong, that the kick bounced off his leg, without moving him at all.

In amazement Ron stopped and yelled to me: "Did you see that! I'm going to fight that?" Quickly Steven stepped over to Ron as he was looking at me for sympathy. Steven pick Ron up like Bolo had done to one of his victims in Enter the Dragon. As Steven was squeezing Ron's abs to his thighs, Ron was screaming. Steven then let his left arm go and held Ron by his legs. Ron was dangling with a fish. After this match Ron nicknamed Steven "Mountain That Does Not Move."

*

1974 original book pictures

There was a misunderstanding that Summer of 1974. A Karate student had heard that I stated Karate was no good. I didn't state this, but this misunderstanding set a crazy incident into motion. Some martial artists had come to visit my class at Jefferson Community Center with violence in mind. They brought a gun, knives, nunchakus and even a samurai sword. They came too early before my evening class. A note was left at the front counter and being from someone who had a bad reputation, I knew something was "not right."

During my class, I was visited by several of the well known martial artists in Seattle. I had never met any of these instructors, but I had heard of them. I had my class doing drills, as I met the instructors on the other side of the room. They were a mix of Karate and Kung-Fu instructors and they tried to speak to me, counseling me that all martial arts are good and that there should be peace between the styles. I was in shock. I explained that I never made such statements. They believed me. One of the instructors that came earlier that day, calmed down. We shook hands and there was peace.

Later that evening my girlfriend and I bumped into that particular instructor and his friends at Imperial Lanes. He was friendly and we spoke about his Karate training. At that time he mentioned that there was also a 5th degree black belt that was going to come up to Seattle to deal with me, if things had not worked out. I was in further shock as I couldn't believe all this over reaction due to a misunderstanding and little old me.

*

1975 Front Kick at Seward Park

Good Kung-Fu instructors were hard to find. In 1975 two guys from Auburn, Washington would drive up to meet me in Chinatown and pick me up from Aya's restaurant on 6th and Main. My girlfriend Cindy worked there. With the crazy 70s Kung-Fu thirst, Dan and Terry drove from Auburn to pick me up and then drove to the Green River Community College Gym, so I could teach them my brand of Kung-Fu. After the class, they would drive me back to Aya's, and then return back to their homes in Auburn.

At first this was kind of tough, as Dan would drive his Corvette. Squeezing three guys into a sports car with two seats and driving from Chinatown to Auburn and back was not fun. They switched cars and it became a bearable ride. We did this for a few months and then I had to quit teaching them because I was spending too much time away from my college books.

*

My brother Steven was preparing to perform some Kung-Fu techniques with some friends for a school function. He came down to my bedroom to practice a few techniques with me to prepare for this event. I remember trying to show him a stop kick. I told him to throw a front kick at me. He threw a powerful back leg front kick, and I threw out a right lead stop side kick. My stop kick landed on his right shin and I was lifted up, landing three feet away from where I started. He had heavy power!

*

I was at Cindy's work one evening. She worked at Aya's, a restaurant on 6th and Main. There was an old customer who was about to light up his cigarette (you could smoke in restaurants back in the 1970s). Cindy just finished lighting the cigarette and then I told her to hold the match. With a quick punch the match was blown out by the wind it created. The customer was certain I blew it out with my mouth and it was a trick. He had me do it again another two times before he believed that the punch itself blew out the match.

*

I was a rookie when it came to tournaments. My friend George Nakauye told me about an upcoming tournament. He stated it was a pretty good one and it would be a good one for my first tournament. This was the 1975 Washington Karate Association Championships. It was Julius Thiry and Akio Minakami's annual tournament. I entered it believing George, but did not understand tournament protocol. The most basic one was it was an invitational, and I was not invited. Did George set me up? I filled out the registration form at the gym and seemed to be the only Kung-Fu person there.

I wore a navy blue, satin Kung-Fu uniform that my sister made for me. My Kung-Fu boots were all leather, custom made in Hong Kong. My father had them made when he visited there a year earlier. At the tournament site, I was a shiny navy blue spot, in a sea of white Karate uniforms.

I was nervous as I didn't what to do, whom to bow to, how to line up, or even what the normal course of events would be. I was signed up for the black belt division for hand kata and weapons kata, for my first tournament. As I was warming up, and practicing my form, I could hear murmurs like "Did you see that Kung-Fu guy?" My girlfriend Cindy and brother Steven were there to give me support.

I lined up with the other black belts and waited for my turn to perform my hand form. It was comical as I followed the actions of the Karate black belts, when to bow, how to line up and when to go up. I performed my "free form" hand form and was sure that I took last place. My techniques looked nothing like Shito-Ryu Karate.

Then it came to the weapons kata. There were fewer black belts and most participants were doing a sai kata. One black belt was doing a bo kata, and I was doing sickles. My razor sharp Japanese sickles were gardening tools I purchased from Toshiro Hardware. These were razor sharp. I remember when I first got them; Cindy wouldn't let me practice without the cardboard blade covers on. She was very smart!

I got up to perform my sickle form and bowed to the judges. I then finger rolled my sickles into action. My "free form" technique was fluid, fast and flawless. The techniques were based on Chinese double saber techniques and the Karate people had never seen anything like it. To my surprise I won the black belt weapons division.

We only had one car and my brother Steven was going to drive Cindy to work, and come back up to pick me up. I gave Steven my sickles and off they went. Then the other black belts started talking about the evening event. It was explained to me that all the black belt winners were to demonstrate their winning forms. There would be other demonstrations as well.

I went to Julius and apologized and explained that I sent my sickles off with my brother. He laughed as he shook his head. Later that night I received my trophy for first place and a kiss on the cheek from that year's Miss Washington State. Winning the division was a great affirmation that my skills, through informal training with my father and developing my own style, could compete with seasoned Karate black belts.

*

I arrived at Imperial Lanes (formerly nicknamed Asian Lanes) and there was a crowd of 20 or so people outside. I knew most of them. One of my friends walked up to me and said: "Lets spar." I replied: "You know you're going to lose." He then said: "I got something for you this time."

My friend was always sparring with me. He had not won a friendly sparring match before, so I found this quite puzzling why he would want to spar in front of a crowd of people we knew. He walked away from me exposing his back, for a moment. I walked towards him, knowing that my quick reflexes should be able to overcome his surprise attack. As he quickly turned around, he extended his arm and in his hand was a loaded 38 Special snub nose revolver. When he turned around, he was reaching for the concealed handgun.

As soon as I saw the revolver rising up, I deflected it with a right hand slap block, I immediately flowed into a right hand five finger dot to his face and eyes. I stopped my strike an inch from his eyes and face. However, when I slap blocked the revolver out of the way, it ended up pointing directly in the face of his friend standing off to the right side.

Once the crowd saw what had happened, they voiced their displeasure with the handgun stunt. They reprimanded him for making a poor, very dangerous choice and situation.

*

In 1976, I took over George Nakauye's lease for the Columbia City location. It was the first time going to an office and signing my life away to rent space for a martial arts school. This martial arts site was different. I had mostly young students, ranging from 14 to 18 years old. These young students were very interested in training in Kung-Fu and worked hard to strengthen their bodies, as well as develop speed and learn this ancient art.

I remember my brother's best friend Darryl Easter taking classes. Back in those days, I had students sparring from the beginning. At that time of my young martial arts career, I was only 19 years old. I remember one day I had Darryl spar against a student named Vincent. He was a muscular wrestler from Rainier Beach High School. As they started to spar, Vincent struck Darryl in the face. I halted the action with concern for injuries and warned Vincent: "No head contact!" He nodded confirming he understood.

I started them up again, and within seconds, Darryl was struck in the face again. I again halted the action and told Vincent directly not to make facial contact. He said: "Yes!" and was ready to resume again. I started them up again, and within seconds he struck Darryl a third time. I loudly yelled: "Stop!" They both stopped sparring and I quickly directed them: "Bow out! Vincent 100 pushups!" He complained slightly, but complied. He never attended class again.

I have had my "problem students" and at the Columbia City school I remember one in particular. I don't remember his name, but I remember two situations with this problem child. He was a 16 year old that had studied Karate in California. He had studied with me for approximately a month. One day he came to class being rude. I said that he had to respect his classmates. He responded: "I can beat everyone here and I could even give you a pretty good fight!" I was incensed by his lack of respect. I asked: "Would you like to spar now? He said: "Yes!"

We walked to the floor and bowed to each other. We were both in a right lead stance. I quickly grabbed his extended right arm with my right hand. My left leg sweep shot out and connected with his right lead leg. His leg flew upward and he was airborne. Before he could hit the floor, I shot out a left sun fist to the right side of his head. He landed on his butt and stayed there, sitting, frozen from the sun fist strike. I was still disgusted with him and abruptly bowed to my disrespectful opponent, still sitting on the floor.

A couple of weeks went by and this disrespectful student was at it again. This time he brought an ugly nunchaku to class. The weapon looked like he had made it from two pieces of 2 x 4 studs that he had rounded into a rough oval shape by using a machete. He used heavy garden twine instead of a sturdy rope to connect the two pieces of wood, as he was wildly spinning these sticks around; his fellow classmates were rushing to get away from him. I stated that he should not spin the weapon near other students. He replied: "I don't care I like these. With these sticks I can take anybody, even you."

He again showed great disrespect. I asked: "Would you let me use that towel?" He laughed and said: "Sure." I took the white sports towel and rolled it up. We again walked to the floor. Right after bowing to each other, he started doing a figure eight with the ugly nunchakus. He was trying to keep me from moving in and attacking him. I snapped the rolled up towel into the twine of his sticks. This immediately stopped the movement of the weapon. I then quickly attacked his chest with three fast punches. He was down. I again bowed to him in disgust. After this incident, he never came back to class.

*

About that time, Dan and Terry came up to meet with me. They had been taking Kung-Fu from the Burien satellite school of Seattle Kung-Fu Club. They became immersed in that classical Southern Kung-Fu style. They asked if I could do a Kung-Fu demonstration in Puyallup. They had a friend that had opened up a Kyokushinkai Karate Dojo, but the local Karate instructors gave him a bad time and threatened to beat him up and close his school.

I went to the South Hill Kung-Fu Academy and performed my demonstration. All the students were impressed and everyone wanted me to be the instructor. The owners were black belt Gary and his wife Nancy, were certain that I were to teach there everything would work out great. I was still in university jail and not focused enough on school. I was trying, but my ADD/ADHD was making college very tough.

I thanked the owners, but declined to teach. They kept calling me back and offered me more money. Each time they did this it was getting harder to say no. Finally Nancy called me and stated that they would pay me $21 per hour and I would have use of their car for commuting. I finally agreed and started teaching there. We never had a complaint, or challenge from any school.

I remember one student named Gary. I had been performing my "double flying side kick" which was very unusual, but very cool. I would take three running steps and throw my body horizontally to the heavy bag. Both feet would strike the bag at the same time, at about the height of my chest. The 85 pound heavy bag would go flying. I would then land on my hands and feet like a cat, as the heavy bag would race back in my direction, speeding over my head.

I only taught on Tuesdays and Thursdays, but the school was also open on Saturdays. One student named Gary decided to try doing my special "double flying side kick." He was not supervised and copied my movements and flew to the bag. He impacted the bag and sent it flying; however, he did not land on his hands and feet as I did. He landed on his hands only. He ended up breaking both wrists and had to remove himself from the class.

Months went by and unfortunately, ego got in the way. The owner was a first degree black belt and didn't want to be a student again. His Karate skills were not good enough to keep him from being harassed by other Karate instructors, but learning from someone else left him feeling without control. Thus our relationship became strained. A few months later, I stopped teaching there and the school soon disappeared.

*

There was a tournament up in the north end of Seattle in 1976. I remember it was a Kenpo tournament. I remember completing in the black belt weapons division. Sensei Akio Minakami was competing in the same division. He was dressed in a hakama and was going to perform a samurai sword. I approached him and greeted him. He remembered me and stated, "You won my tournament last year. You are very good." I thanked him and we both prepared for our division to start.

There were a few notable instructors Jerry Gould, Roger Tung and Akio Minakami. The other black belt participants were a less known. Jerry performed sickles, Roger did a saber form, Akio performed samurai sword, and I performed double two foot sticks. In the end Jerry took first place, Roger took second place, I can't remember who took third, but I ended up taking fourth-place.

*

Later in the spring of 1976, I competed in Jerry Gould's West Coast Regional. This tournament had black belt hard weapons, as well as black belt soft weapons. I entered in this division with Roger Tung, my brother-in-law's older brother Albert Lee, and a novice black belt level practitioner. The main competition was between Roger and me. I was still competing with the double sticks, even though an instructor friend told me to use flashier weapons.

I remember they had a tough time trying to come up with enough black belt soft stylists to judge the division. Back in those days there weren't very many black belt level Kung-Fu people. So they just started asking anybody who might have trained a little bit in Kung-Fu but was a black belt.

Roger was up first and did a very good saber form. It was a typical Roger Tung form, very flashy, and with great technique. I was up second and performed my double oak sticks with speed, and fluid power. My form was impressive and flawless that was until the last second. As I was performing the finger roll to bow out, this stick in my right hand got loose and spun, dropping to the floor. The sound of this stick impacting the wood floor was deafening. I caught this stick on the second bounce close to the floor. As I looked up I saw small smile on Roger's face. He knew that with a small mistake he was in first place.

*

One day at the Columbia City school, Cindy and I were the last two left. We were doing a bit of sparring and then a group of three people walked in. It was a grandfather, father and young son. The father started asking about classes and I gave him the classes schedule and fee. He stated that he wanted his son to take lessons and that had himself learned from a Shaolin Monk. At that point he struck himself in the head a few times. I wasn't impressed. This was 1976, and few if any Shaolin Monks could be found at all.

He then wanted to show me what he had taught his son. I was trying to be cordial, and watched for a while. There didn't seem to be any apparent technique. The father was just punching at the 10 year old, and the child was trying to block the strikes.

After five minutes of this, I said: "Okay, I understand what your son can do. We have to close up now, so when you're ready please come back and sign up for class." The father kept trying to keep us there at the school, but Cindy and I had plans. Finally he got the message that we needed to leave, but he was not pleased.

He closed his eyes and put his hands on his stomach. I asked: "Excuse me, what are you doing?" He stated: "I'm challenging you!" I replied: "Sorry, I don't accept challenges." He hesitated, thought about it for a second and then left with his family. Cindy and I couldn't believe this strange encounter. Yes, just another day in a Kung-Fu school on Rainier.

The Path of Least Resistance

I remember an incident that involved my father and me during that busy summer of 1974. My father came down to my room and was not happy with me not being around the house so much. I had a girlfriend and I was always trying to be with her. He complained that I had to do my chores and stay at the house more often. As a typical teenager, I said yes to everything, but he must have sensed that I really didn't agree with what he had to say.

My father had a bad temper. He walked up stairs and then something set him off. He quickly ran down the stairs and punched my semi-closed door open. He stated that I had better take him seriously. He then said: "If you think you can take old dad, you got something coming to you!" He then walked up the stairs and then left for work.

I was very upset. I hadn't thought of my dad threatening me and getting into a physical fight. I felt I was a better martial artist than my father at that time. I couldn't believe he wanted fight with me. Actually he would have won. I was more athletic and could do more techniques, but my father had fighting experience and he was meaner than me.

I felt the only option at that point was to move out. In essence "run away from home."

I told Cindy about the situation and she made a call to her father. He agreed that I could move in to his apartment in the Central District. I packed up my clothes, archery equipment, Kung-Fu weapons and my shotguns, and drove to the apartment in my sister's Buick.

I remember calling my sister at her work. She was the assistant manager at the time at Bon Marche. Telling her what I was doing, she advised against it, but I stated that I had made up my mind. I delivered all my possessions and drove her Buick back to my parents' house. I left it in the driveway.

Cindy and I received a ride down to her mother's home in the Rainier Valley, and we started to get dinner ready. No one else was in the house, just the two of us. Hours after I had told Susan what I was doing, the doorbell rang. I heard the husband of my mother's best friend ask if I was there. Cindy tried explaining the situation to him. I heard my mother crying and I couldn't help myself, I walked into the living room and saw her.

She immediately ran to me crying and asking me to come back home. I started crying and told her that I couldn't because of my father's anger. Many emotions came out and I agreed to go back home.

I arrived later that night, back to my home where all this drama started. I saw my father and I could tell he was upset too. Feeling guilty he said: "Silly boy, all I did was just scold you." Everything went back to being normal after that.

My sister later told me that she had called and told our mother what was happening right after I called her. My mother called her best friend letting her know of the situation. The only driver was the best friend's husband. The three of them rode out to block the Buick in the driveway. Once they found out I was already gone. They made calls all over the place. How they found out where Cindy lived, I still don't know to this day.

My sister also mentioned something that was significant. She told me that our father was possibly feeling bad that he was losing his son, and hunting and fishing buddy. I was surprised as that never occurred to me.

*

I believe this incident and my mother's teachings of not creating "trouble" had me programmed not to "rock the boat." The path of least resistance would be not to be there for the fight. I believe that this programming has had me not confront those that needed to put in their place, or to explain myself fully in matters of conflict.

I have held back as I knew that it was okay for me to swallow my tongue, rather than to have total war. If we had total war, things would not be pretty and no one would be unscathed. If I accepted the B.S., then at least we could get through the situation. This occurred with several of my problem students, my job with the Seattle Department of Parks and Recreation and other situations over the years.

Total Peace, or Total War

My philosophy has always been total peace, or total war. It is far better to work towards peace than to go to fight. I have always taught my students in martial arts and firearms, to avoid confrontation at all cost. When you need to defend yourself, there can only be total war, as you are defending your life. Any other situation should be dealt with avoidance. Better to swallow your pride, than to be put in a situation that is final.

I have always taught my students there is no such thing as jumping in a stance, or hitting a person a couple of times and then leaving. You never show your pistol and then walk away. I stated that real life is not a John Wayne movie. There is no situation where you get in a fight and later have a drink with your antagonist.

Real Kung-Fu and firearms are serious business. Use it only if you have to and it better be a life, or death situation. Knowing this, everyone does everything they can for a peaceful solution, to avoid the act of total war and probable death.

*

My son Jason had met a girl that was single at the time. She had just broken up with her boyfriend. Jason went out with her for a very short time, and then the couple got back together. Jason felt the girl used him to make her boyfriend jealous. The boyfriend ended up going crazy and would contact Jason and threaten him. Jason filed charges against him with Kent and Bellevue Police. The young man was still harassing Jason whenever he could.

One Friday Brandon (then a teenager) spent the night at the hospital for dehydration. I stayed the night with Brandon to keep him company and help him. We got home the next day at about 1:00 p.m. We both were exhausted and went to sleep. Waking up about 8:00 p.m. we went about our normal activities.

At 1:00 a.m. Sunday morning, we heard a big crash. I was upstairs and was worried Brandon fell. Brandon was downstairs and thought something happened to me. We both arrived at the middle level of the house, each asking the other if they were okay. Neither one of us fell, or broke something, so I looked around. I found a large garden brick had been thrown through my front window.

Going outside I noticed that two bricks had been thrown at the same time. One made it through the window and the second bounced off the aluminum frame. I looked around and noticed an empty box of five dozen Safeway eggs sitting in the middle of the street. I looked at my house and noticed Jason's room, peppered with all those eggs. Right there and then, I realized it was that crazy jealous boyfriend and his friends.

A report was filed with the King County Sheriff's Department. The inefficiency of the police resulted in no consequences to the immature boyfriend. I did want to go to the boy's parents, but decided to use the police. Had the boys confronted me while they were carrying out this crime, there could have been very serious consequences. If I had to defend myself from a few immature, aggressive idiots with bricks in their hands, they may have ended up maimed, or dead. They were lucky that that I did not pursue the issue, and be placed in a situation where I would have to defend myself. I believed that though the result of this situation was not positive and justice was not served, a peaceful ending was achieved.

*

About five years ago Jason was assaulted on Tyee High School's outdoor basketball court. He was playing a pickup game and stole the ball from a large 6'3" Samoan. As Jason went up to lay the ball in, the other player pushed Jason into the pole supporting the backboard. Jason was in immense pain. He slowly got up and the perpetrator extended his hand and asked if it was cool. Jason pushed his hand away and said: "Just play ball."

Shortly after that, Jason was running up the court, the other player suddenly turned around and punched Jason in the head. Stunned Jason stood there and the perpetrator landed another punch. Jason fell down onto the cement court. Then the perpetrator and his friend mercilessly kicked Jason in his upper body and head. A young lady was waiting to get on the court and saw this incident. She immediately called the police, and the attackers fled the scene.

I met Jason at the hospital. He had bleeding from his kidney due to the impact with the support pole. His right eye was completely shut and the orbital lobe was crushed. His left eye would only open about half way. There was bruising everywhere.

When Jason healed up, I suggested going back to the court to look for the attacker. All I wanted to do was to video tape him and his vehicle. I would then print pictures and hand them over to the police so they could put this violent criminal in jail. Jason was reluctant, but we did go out there once.

The situation was probably too traumatic for Jason and I did not pursue this any further.

My Early Fears

My lack of ability to speak Cantonese was always something that haunted me in the back of my mind. I spoke Toisonese, but this dialect was not often used. Whenever someone asked me if I spoke Chinese, they replied with a slight pompous air "Oh" when I stated I only spoke Toisonese. These people actually needed to communicate in Cantonese and not in English. Their English skills were probably lacking and they didn't realize they were being rude. However, my experiences with Sifus from Southern China, have been positive. I believe their mutual respect for other martial artists, is much greater than the respect of the common person.

I remember going to the Western Canadian Chinese Martial Arts Association Banquet one year. My good friend Ken Low invited me. I felt awkward as though I was Chinese, I couldn't communicate with the immigrant Sifus lacking English skills. Being a second generation American Chinese, I knew communication was going to be difficult. I also didn't know what to expect.

I sat at a table with a Sifu in his seventies. He was very nice to me and though we could not communicate, we got through the dinner with unspoken understanding. We offered each other various dishes. He respected me as a young instructor from the U.S. and I respected him as my elder and as an older uncle in Kung-Fu.

*

When I was young, I knew I had quite a bit of ability, but in the back of my mind I would sometimes have self doubt. I sometimes thought sure I could do this and that, but was I as good as other Kung-Fu instructors? They had more experience and they also had history and legacy on their side.

Several of my students had experience with other instructors and I was happy to find out that I was similar in ability as some of these famous instructors. I also had the opportunity to see other famous instructors perform at tournaments and believed that my abilities were comparable.

As I had more success in the 1980s, I became part of the established Seattle martial arts community. I had been creating our own history and legacy all that time.

Mean People Who Thought They Knew Kung-Fu

One day while practicing at the Kung-Fu Club as a sophomore at Cleveland High School, a stranger came to the class. One of our high school seniors that spoke Cantonese conversed with him. This little guy from Hong Kong looked at me and said something to the senior, who translated: "He wants to beat you up." I smiled and all I could think of was: "Right…" He didn't pursue it, and nothing happened. But he was one of numerous individuals who thought just because they knew a little Kung-Fu, they were tough, and were great fighters.

Another participant at the Kung-Fu Club also learned a little Kung-Fu while he lived in Hong Kong. One day when we were discussing techniques, he offered to show me what he was trying to explain. However, he threw me to the floor and promptly apologized for the accident. I knew it was no accident. He was just a jerk, with no honor or integrity. Even though it would have been satisfying I let him go. I knew I shouldn't repay the favor.

Six years later, I was at a Chinese restaurant in North Seattle having dinner with my future wife. The waiter had met me once before, as we had a mutual friend. Somehow, he overheard my date and I discussing my private Kung-Fu class that I was teaching and he interrupted: "Oh my Kung-Fu is better that his, but he is a gun expert!" Now when did he mentally probe my mind and ascertain that his skill and knowledge was greater than mine? Hmmmmm.

These were "wanna be" martial artists and people who thought they were better than they really were. I thought this was just an innate trait until I met real Chinese Sifus and quality practitioners like my Sifu friends from Canada and Seattle, who demonstrated friendship, honor and integrity.

1974-1975 Creation of Yee Jong Kune Do

In my senior year of high school, my Kung-Fu practice was at an all time high. I spent three, to four hours a day practicing. I started to write and draw out forms that I created. In my mind, I wanted to practice application. I felt at that time, a style could be limited to one form. That expanded to two and then three. I wanted to have the form based on classical Chinese techniques. My main philosophy at the time was "free form." I could instantaneously do a series of impromptu Kung-Fu movements that created a new form each time.

This was hard to explain because most martial artists could only perform forms only in a set manner. Many people who claimed to be "free form," but their movements were not fluid, flowing and natural.

My belief was that if one could freely use techniques in a flowing, continuous fashion, then the real world application would be just as easy in self defense and combat. My belief also differed from Bruce Lee's. His philosophy was to learn techniques and then strip away what was not useful. My belief was to learn many techniques and understand them. One could use their "best" techniques, but if they failed you would also have many more to try.

My combat stance would emphasize the strong side lead. This was due to the philosophy of Wing Chun. The strong side lead differs from 99% of the martial arts out there. Most martial art systems have the weak hand out to block and defend against an attack. They reserve the strong hand to deliver powerful blows. In contrast my style emphasizes using the coordinated, strong, fast hand as the lead. This gives the individual the best weapon forward to defend, or attack. The weak hand is the "second gate" and is more powerful than it usually is, by use of shoulder, or hip movement to add to the power.

I worked on my drawings to lay out my initial form and kept them in an old blue binder. It was to be the only form and all other practice would be "free form" and application practice. This first form became what our current students now know as Jong Hop Kune. I decided I should lay out an easier form and one more complex. I developed these two other forms, but never taught them to anyone.

In 1975 my friend Wayne Chan, a Hong Kong immigrant, was helping me name my unnamed style. Wayne was a Goju Karate practitioner. He stated he took Karate instead of Kung-Fu, because in Hong Kong it was less costly.

Naming something well is critical in any culture especially to the Chinese. For a few months we hashed out many possibilities to identify a name for my style with the essence of my art in mind. He came up with two possibilities. One was Yee Kune Do, Cantonese for the Way of the Mind (or Intellectual) Fist. The other was Jong Kune Do - the Way of the Combination Fist. I liked both names, and told Wayne I wanted to use the names combined. My style would be called Yee Jong Kune Do.

Wayne didn't like it and told me this was not done. Most Chinese names of styles only had three words. To use four words would be "unlucky," as four characters could be viewed with the relationship of "sei." This Cantonese word means four, but it also sounds like the word for death. I liked it though and still wanted use Yee Jong Kune Do. I used an abstract meaning for Yee, as I wanted to imply it was my internal feelings/knowledge that would adapt to my external challenges and environment. The name grew on Wayne. Thus, Yee Jong Kune Do was officially born.

My style was classical, yet non-classical. It was seeded in generations of Chinese martial arts, but able to adapt to modern needs and philosophies. Classical movements were effective. If you never experienced them, countering them would be tough. Being open minded and having an eye for what works guided this practical style.

I used the spelling of "Kune" rather than "Chuan." Kune is a spelling of the Cantonese word for fist or style. Chuan, "Chwan," was used in many older books but is the Mandarin word for fist, or style. Bruce Lee's spelling of Kune can be seen in his style of Jeet Kune Do. Other Kung-Fu styles and instructors from Hong Kong had also used the spelling "Kuen."

I created our symbol The Yee Jong Kune Do symbol in 1974 after collecting various martial arts books about other styles. I studied their movements to understand potential opponents' strength and weaknesses. I studied their philosophies to understand in a broader sense, the related techniques and ideology.

One book that I purchased in 1974 was a book on Shorinji Kempo. It was the Japanese version of Sil Lum (Shaolin) Kung-Fu. This book had an interesting symbol with a circle and four curved lines quartering the circle. I liked its symmetry. As I applied the philosophical ideas of my combination Kung-Fu style to it, I vastly changed it, and it transformed the symbol to describe the true essence of my Kung-Fu.

The Yee Jong Kune Do symbol is the official icon of Yee Jong Pai Kung-Fu. This graphic has very special meaning to practitioners of Yee Jong Pai martial arts, therefore; you must understand the meaning behind it.

1. The outer circle of the YJKD symbol symbolizes completeness and the comprehensive nature of the YJKD philosophy.

2. The inner circle of the YJKD symbol represents fluidity and circular technique.

3. The three lines of the triangle represent angular fighting, linear technique and the pillars of the YJKD fighting philosophy: speed, power and accuracy. Each of these qualities are vitally important to developing effective fighting skills. However, if they are not equally balanced then your technique will be less than optimal.

4. At the heart of the YJKD symbol is the modified yin/yang icon, which represents seemingly contradictory yet complimentary concepts (i.e. hard and soft, light and dark, male and female). In this version of the famous double fish symbol, there are four fish heads instead of two, giving the feeling of continuous motion, fluidity and constant change. The underlying concept is that one continues to react to change by changing. For example, if you look at one of the black heads, you can take it to symbolize a hard weapon, attack or energy. However, if you cover that part of the symbol and move counter clockwise 45 degrees, you flow into a white fish head which you can take to mean the flowing from hard to soft. Move 45 degrees again, and you return to the hard attack or defense or weapon or energy. Now you can begin to see the true flowing nature of the symbol and therefore, the real philosophy of Yee Jong Kune Do. Also note that the fish flow counter clockwise. The original yin-yang symbol flows clockwise, to symbolize energy flowing into you. In Yee Jong Pai, however, we want the energy to flow from us and into our opponents.

1979 Ling Ghek Gwun / Double Nunchakus

Slowing Down My Reflexes

I know this sounds funny, but I had to slow my reflexes down. As I trained more, my reactions were too fast and I was too jumpy. My reactions were to instinctively counter attack against any aggressive action or surprises.

*

Once when I was in Junior High School, I was using the downstairs bathroom in my parent's home. I had just opened the door and took a step out, when suddenly something flew by my face. I instinctively turned 180 degrees and shot out a punch. It happened so fast that I didn't know who was there. My punch landed on my brother's mouth.

1979 Flying Front Kick

*

As a 7th grader at Asa Mercer Junior High, I was once talking to my friend Noel Eguchi. From nowhere he flicked out his stiletto with a 7" blade. Just as it snapped and the blade locked, I instinctively punched Noel in the chest. He dropped the knife at my fist's impact. He then got mad at me because other people would have backed off and been afraid. Weird.

*

One day just before practicing at the high school Kung-Fu Club during my sophomore year, I noticed my friend Kevin Rice wasn't at the locker room like he usually was. So, I grabbed my bag and went to my normal last locker on the last row. I tried lifting the handle, but it seemed stuck. So, I used two hands to lift up on the handle, and the door swung open. Kevin was hiding inside the locker and shouted: "Boo!" At the same time he moved his hands to scare me. He was successful! I automatically shot out a left handed Sun fist, that landed squarely on Kevin's nose. He swore at me, bleeding profusely. My heart raced and pounded so strong it felt it was in my throat.

All the jocks in the locker room knew of what had happened. I apologized to Kevin and everything seemed to cool down. Some of them kept talking about what had happened and made negative comments about what I did.

My friend Raphael Marion told the other guys in the gym: "Allen's cool because he knows all that Kung-Fu stuff and he doesn't mess with anybody. If it was me, I'd be kicking everybody's ass!" The guys laughed and that was that.

*

One day I was at Franklin High School visiting my girlfriend Cindy. I didn't see her and began to chat with our mutual friends. A few minutes later I felt a choke hold beginning to go around my neck. As the arm started to tighten, I immediately shot out a backward elbow strike. I didn't know it was Cindy. Luckily, as soon as I reacted, she let go and moved sideways. My quick elbow strike struck her full length denim coat and narrowly missed her ribs.

*

The last incident was on my 21st birthday. I was visiting my sister and brother-in-law at their apartment. They lived in the Muana Kai Apartments on North side of Beacon Hill. I pushed the button to bring the elevator down to the first floor. As the elevator doors opened, I took a step forward. At the same time a nice gentleman in his mid-thirties and in a three-piece suit took a step to exit the elevator. I instinctively shot out a high/low sun fist strike. As the fists were racing to the man's chest and stomach, I caught myself, realizing there was no threat. I slowed the fists as they touched the man's body. I stated in a soft, apologetic voice: "I'm so sorry!" He was as surprised and shocked as me. He said it was okay. We both left the scene.

1979 Saber

Luck and Its Effect On Self Defense and Creation of Martial Arts Styles

There is a huge amount of skill when it comes to effective self defense. One has to develop speed, power and accuracy of movement, to effectively counter attacks thrown by an aggressor. Skill is the main ingredient for success. However, good, or bad luck of trying to deflect or block an attack can sometimes be huge factor in the outcome. Luck does happen. When bad luck strikes you can miss a block. This can mean defeat. With good luck and the opponent can't touch you.

Once a full contact fight from Hong Kong was on the Wide World of Sports on ABC, one Saturday afternoon in the late 70s. They featured a. The fight was between Ron Van Cleef, a Goju Karate expert and actor and a White Crane stylist from Central Europe. Ron was huge, very muscular and much faster than the White Crane stylist. Ron hit and kicked his opponent at will. He seemed so fast and smooth that the opponent didn't have a chance. Suddenly dropped down to do a leg scissor around his opponent's knee and ankle.

1979 Double Sickles

Bad luck struck! Ron's leg scissor did not go far enough to get any leverage. Instead of getting out of the failed technique, Ron continued to hang on to the White Crane stylist's lead leg. What happened next was unfathomable. The opponent turned and used his back leg to deliver a roundhouse kick to Ron's face. Ron was knocked out so completely that his limp body did not move for three, or four minutes. The weaker, slower, less experienced fighter won.

Luck also is a factor in creating martial arts styles. In the 70s and 80s, many styles of martial arts were created. Good luck helped in selecting effective techniques and philosophies that would make or break a new style. People naming a style "Wombat Karate" or something similar, would be at a disadvantage from the get go. Performing techniques that were not effective or not displaying speed, power and focus, would also be a disaster.

In 1974 my original concept was that my style would have one form. Everything else would be free style forms with intense development of individual fighting techniques. Soon after, I decided that an easier fundamental form should be included. Then I created a more complex form. Six years later, due to my students' interests, I created animal forms and techniques.

I developed the philosophy of eight animals and eight methods and taught these forms and techniques accordingly. I created Baat Ying Baat Faat (Eight Animals Eight Methods), and soon after created Yhien Dhoy Ghin Suk (Modern Warfare). With a talented student who had specific technique needs, I created Luk Ying Duin Dah (Six Animal Short Strikes).

I have been very creative all these years, but I was also lucky in my choices and fortunate with how I followed through. I could easily have stopped my progression in 1974. Had I stopped, my relationships with all the various Sifus in the Pacific Northwest would have changed. Students would not have competed in forms divisions. Animal techniques would not have been developed to their current level of complexity.

With different choices, Yee Jong Kune Do may have never progressed into Yee Jong Pai. Baat Ying Baat Faat, Yhien Dhoy Ghin Suk and Luk Ying Duin Dah may never have come to be.

So lady luck can be an important factor when it comes to choices, self defense, combat, and the creation of martial art styles.

Mother-in-law Peggy Mitchell

1980 Kent school students

1980 Creation of Techniques Based On the Spirit of the Individual Animal

Prior to 1980 my Kung-Fu techniques were a huge bank of various striking, kicking and blocking techniques. I knew several animal techniques and, more importantly, how to apply them.

In 1980 my students told me they wanted to learn more traditional Kung-Fu animal techniques. This led them to classical Kung-Fu animal techniques. When I started to teach the various animal techniques to my students, they wanted more. They loved learning specific animal techniques and how to apply them, but they also wanted forms.

From their requests, I realized something that distinguished my approach. Some Chinese martial art styles taught an animal technique or two, and then combine typical blocks, strikes and kicks to that form. What I realized which was different was that the animal form must use techniques specific to that animal. I further thought that each animal has its own spirit. Movements should be pure - done with that philosophy in mind.

Thus our animal forms use animal weapons specific to that particular animal with movements of the perceived individual spirit in mind.

Leopard Technique

Monkey Technique

Tiger Technique

Side kick variations from the 1980 Beacon Hill School

Bellevue Kung-Fu Club

With the encouragement of my sister, I opened the Bellevue Kung-Fu Club in the fall 1982. I ran a couple small newspaper ads to recruit new students. My first student at that location was Bruce Friedman, a teenager who lived near my sister's house in Bellevue.

1982 Factoria Square Mall Demonstration

The school was about 1,300 square feet. I believe it was originally a fireplace shop. A big uncarpeted square towards the back of the room was likely where the main fireplace display unit stood. I placed a green colored piece of carpet there for a sparring square. Though it was a little tight for general sparring, it was great to teach sparring in close quarters.

This school was very unique because it permitted students to practice things they would not find in other schools. We had hay bales for archery practice and a bullet trap was in the back room for air rifles and pistols. We even had 36" diameter log for throwing stars and throwing knives.

*

One of my early Bellevue Kung-Fu Club students was Jack Mattison. He nicknamed himself the Gray Tiger. He and his friend Dave McKinney used to come down from North Bend to attend class. Jack drove his "Green Monster," an old green Chevy Suburban. He brought a gang of kids with him too. Jack's daughter Sheri, Dave's children Mark, Karla and Caroline, and teenagers that were recruited by Jack. They all arrived in the "Green Monster." They were great students, always enthusiastic about learning and training.

Part of what made Jack a great student was his constant wondering about new solutions to different self defense circumstances. He knew from experience that if he asked a question, I would demonstrate how to counter the movement on him. Jack started to use the "Jedi Mind Trick" on the younger students in class. He would question: "I wonder how Sifu would get out of that?" The student standing next to him would start to think and say: "Yes, I wonder how he would he get out of that?" When the younger student asked me, I would demonstrate on him. One day I caught on went directly to demonstrate on Jack.

1983 tea ceremony with Jack Mattison

Jack had a big heart and loved Kung-Fu. He wanted to continue to push himself and learn our energetic Baat Ying Baat Faat (Eight Animals Eight Methods) style. He loved the fast, fluid, powerful animal techniques. However, due to his age and injuries to his body, I decided it was best for Jack to learn our Yao Kune (Soft Fist). This was one of the eight methods and was much like Yang Tai Chi.

Jack became a born again Christian. He sailed to different countries on a ship delivering medical supplies. On one such visit to China, he stopped at a local park. He was amazed when he saw all these people practicing Tai Chi. Jack then got the courage to get up there and practice Yao Kune in front of everyone. He performed the short version of the form and noticed several people watching him. At the end of his form, one of the Tai Chi practitioners looked at him smiled and gave a nod. Jack gave a reciprocal nod. When Jack got back he proudly told me the story and stated that this was the first time my style was performed on Chinese soil.

*

In 1983 Nehemiah Sirkis and an Israeli operative visited my school at Factoria Square. Nehemiah was a firearms designer for Detonics Manufacturing. Before working at Detonics Manufacturing he was already a famous firearms designer and also had a history with the Israeli military. The operative was very impressed with my demonstration of Kung-Fu techniques. He commented that I was so natural with weapons and techniques that I must have trained from a very early age.

*

Phyllis Whitbeck was another quality student, an older woman who started in the Bellevue Kung-Fu Club. Phyllis lived in Issaquah, near Bellevue. She liked the class. When I closed down my doors in Bellevue and started working for the Seattle Department of Parks and Recreation, she continued to attend classes in Seattle. Each class she picked up Michael Gibson, Bruce Friedman and Gary Begue in Bellevue and took them to classes with her. Without her support I believe the Bellevue students would not have continued. They owe their learning opportunities to her.

Phyllis liked learning forms and had our first two forms memorized. She was great and had a young mind. She would play our sparring game "Death Chambers" and get other students out with her wit and cunning. This sparring game was held on a basketball court. The sides of the basketball key would be the imaginary walls of the chamber, no one could cross that field. The free throw line would be the entrance of the chamber. A team of Guardians would be in the chamber, but could only have no more than one of their feet past the free throw line. Raiders could enter the chamber only through the front. The team of Raiders would have to fight their way into the chamber to get the treasure (usually a traffic cone) located in the back. The Guardians would defend and protect the treasure and dispatch all invaders.

This point sparring game was always popular and taught speed, accuracy, and concentration with multiple opponents. Phyllis would walk up slowly to the free throw line, just outside the reach of person in front of her. She would wait while numerous kicks and punches would fly. She would wait until the action slowed a bit, then quickly attack an opponent concentrating on someone else. Her surprise attack permitted her to be effective against opponents faster and younger than her.

*

1983 Bellevue Kung-Fu Club double fist drill

Rod McNeil was a tall, 15 year old student from Preston, Washington. One summer day we were working on joint locks. I asked Rod to grab my arm, but he was reluctant, very nervous and tense. I told him to relax, but in a jerky fashion, he grabbed for my arm in a quick downward motion. He violently ripped my Kung-Fu uniform pocket off.

In an odd, quick, reflexive action I shot out a front kick to his groin. Rod lifted off the floor and grabbed his groin. Quickly landing on his knees, he keeled over. I had never done anything like a reflexive kick before, or since this incident. Rod looked like Artie Johnson from Rowan and Martin's Laugh In, the guy always falling over sideways in a tricycle. I apologized for the accidental kick and Rod was fine. From then on he was always relaxed when working on joint locks.

Another incident happened involving Rod. We were working in the sparring square one day. I was teaching a lead hand deflection and hand check followed by a hammer fist strike to the top of head. Rod was the third student to work on this combination. I demonstrated on each student so they could see how the combination worked. As Rod squared off with me I performed the combination on him. I did it quickly, with precision and the hammer fist strike was done lightly.

Rod said: "You can't do that." I stated that I just did it. He stated again that I couldn't do it. So I performed the combination again. Rod then said: "You can't do that, because I don't have the top of my skull." I was now worried as he was struck twice on the top of his head, where there wasn't bone at the top of his skull. Rod's parents never disclosed this condition on his registration forms for my school.

Rod said he felt fine, but then got dizzy and momentarily lost his balance. He again said he was okay. He walked about 30 feet and turned towards me and said: "Sifuuuuuu." Then he fell on the corner edge of my glass showcases. As he fell, I rushed over to him. He started convulsing. His body was tight, and he turned red from not breathing. I stood over him and finally he started breathing. Shortly he regained stability. I asked what was going on in his mind at the time of the fall.

He said that he blacked out, and the next thing he remembered was me standing over him. He said as he looked at my face, my hair shot out and the room turned black. He said that all of a sudden he found himself out in front of the school. A station wagon full of girls drove by him. That's when he started running after the girls. That's when he regained consciousness.

The lesson here is that this incident wouldn't have happened if his medical condition had been properly disclosed. It's funny what a girl crazy teenager sees in his mind when he is unconscious and convulsing.

*

Training was very difficult. At this time period I had students training very hard with a combination of traditional and modern exercises. I had several "one day students" lasted only one day (one class actually). The classes would break down muscles that students didn't know they had.

1983 Bellevue Kung-Fu Club promotional picture

The hour and a half hour class emphasized training in strength, speed and endurance development. Classical forms and movements also was drilled into the students. Weaponry was instructed to students who were more advanced.

The "hard core" training days of the Bellevue Kung-Fu Club, were very tough. Classes were three times harder than they are today. The hard workouts benefited the older teenagers and those adults that were fit enough to survive the classes. Looking back, I wish my classes had been easier for the younger children. I had quite a number of them, but they often trained with the adults. I now realize they could have been more successful if the classes were not as physically challenging.

No Cheers For the big Chinese Guy

In the 1980s I was looking for work as a police officer. I had several friends and customers in law enforcement. Ever since that group incident with the sword, knives, nunchakus and gun I had interest in becoming a policeman.

After completing the physical tests for the cities of Kent and Tukwila. I then decided to do the physical for the King County Sheriff's Department. Their test was held indoors at a high school up North. As I got there I noticed one of the tests was the "shuttle run." In this exercise one had to run, touch a line and then go back touch a farther line and keep repeating this.

Steel Whip Underhand Poke

We used to do this drill in high school for basketball practice. The difference was there was a chalkboard eraser that we had to put in the "tape rectangle" to increase the difficulty. I had been teaching monkey walk and duck walks. My legs were very strong and could do low movements with coordination and strength.

Watching the group in front of mine, I saw a small, wiry, bearded individual finish the shuttle run with his third attempt at 11 seconds. Everyone in his group cheered for his achievement. Our group was up next. Upon my first attempt, I completed it in 11 seconds. Several people looked at me with a confused look, but no one cheered. No love for the big Chinese guy. Knowing that I did a very good time for my first attempt, my next two attempts were slower at 12 and 13 seconds.

Double weapons with Bruce Friedman

The 1980s

In 1980 I had an interest in changing from the firearm industry to law enforcement. I had applied at the Seattle Police Department and a few other agencies. A recruiting officer from the Seattle Police Department named Ty Sheffey contacted me. We met discussed the police department. We talked about my qualifications and my interests. He stated that he studied Karate from one of my friends, but did not like the way upper class-men beat the lower belts. He signed a three month contract but forfeited two months of lessons, because he hated going to class to receive a pounding each time he showed up.

I invited Ty to go to my home to view my Thursday private class. At that time I lived in Kent, and he drove out to see how Kung-Fu was different from Karate. He performed the drills and exercises and saw a difference in the emphasis on movement. I tried showing him how Kung-Fu develops fluid power and the differences in using physical strength. I explained that there were many ways to use effective techniques without the use of overt strength.

Playing chess with Nghia Halpain and carrying young Brandon

I demonstrated a crab claw to his throat. As the pressure of the finger tips closed on his carotid artery, he gagged and tears appeared in his eyes. I explained I applied very little pressure with the crab claw, but two fingers could incapacitate an opponent. He was amazed with this effective technique and was in awe.

A week later he called me up excited about a situation that had happened on the Sunday following the class he attended. He dropped his wife off at Frederick and Nelsons, and he and his son were going to find parking. While driving he saw a woman snatch a purse from a female victim. The woman then ran and passed the purse off to a man. Ty parked the car in the middle of the street and told his son not to move. He ran down the male suspect and grabbed him. They both started to tussle, and out of nowhere he reached up and applied a crab claw to the suspect's neck. To Ty's surprise the man dropped immediately grabbing his throat and coughing. He then handcuffed him. Ty thought I should know about the effectiveness of the technique and that he unintentionally used it to subdue this suspect.

I told Ty that because he was so impressed with the crab claw technique, he subconsciously thought about it. The crab claw came out instinctively much like the legend of how White Crane Kung-Fu was developed by a man seeing a white crane defend itself against an ape. In this story the man seeing the battle was so impressed with the triumphant white crane that he kept thinking about it's movements. When the man was attacked by bandits, he instinctively evaded and attacked just like the white crane.

*

In 1983 I heard from other Kung-Fu instructors that Roger Tung was back in town. He had been to China learning more Wushu. I met him at the Pacific Northwest Ballet training facility where his students were practicing. It was good to see Roger after all those years he had been traveling. He became nationally rated number 1 in soft forms. He showed me several Chinese weapons he'd brought back to sell.

I purchased a couple of 6 ½ foot spears, a couple of steel whips and a straight sword. As light Wushu weapons they were great. Unfortunately, the spears didn't hold up to my heavy use. I broke both wax wood staffs of the spears simply by speed and momentum movements with sudden strikes in the air. They broke off at where my lead hand was. I salvaged the spear heads and placed them on heavier duty wax wood staffs.

 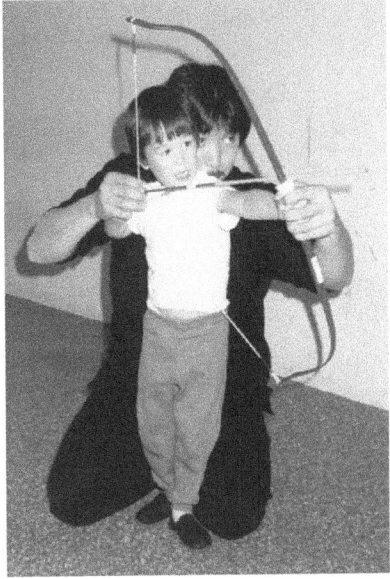

Three year old Jason sparring and shooting a bow on his birthday

*

In 1983 I was contacted to provide a Kung-Fu demonstration at the Chinatown Summer Street Festival. This was the first time I had demonstrated openly in Chinatown. I brought my students to Hing Hay Park and we started to get ready for the two 30 minute demonstrations. After stretching and practicing movements, I grabbed my straight sword and started my fast, fluid movements with it.

Billy Yamamoto, a former student appeared and greeted us. He learned from me in 1974 and at the Kent school in 1980. He said: "I knew that was you when I saw the sword movements and the finger twirling. You're the only one that does it that way." We spoke for a little bit and then I re-focused for the demonstration.

It was a hot summer day and the red bricks of Hing Hay Park radiated heat. While warming up, I stepped on a piece of gum. It was so hot that the gum stuck to the bottom of my Kung-Fu boot, like freshly melted cheese on a pizza. After a quick clean up, we were ready to go.

The demonstration consisted of hand forms, weapon techniques and self defense application. We even brought a large red foam wrestling mat to demonstrate take downs and throws. The demonstration was a success and was well received. We performed twice that day, and we were asked to demonstrate the following year.

1983 Chinatown Summer Street Festival with Dave McKinney and Mike Galanti

1983 my father performing a Choy Li Fut staff form

*

Soon afterwards I was asked to demonstrate at Richard Moton's Kodiak Karate Tournament. I brought Michael Gibson with me for the demonstration. Halfway through the tournament, Richard had us do our demonstration. I explained to the audience that many of the techniques in Chinese Kung-Fu incorporated the movements and the spirit of animals. I demonstrated the animal movements of the crane, tiger, snake and monkey. Then I demonstrated the movements on Michael.

When I performed the monkey style application I got carried away. I grabbed Michael, threw him to the ground and struck at him several times with hammer fists. Then I instinctively did a hair trap. The last movement was an accident. I had ripped Michael's backward baseball cap off. Doing so I had exposed his bright green Mohawk. Michael was going through a punk stage at the time. Half the audience gasped. The other half laughed.

After the audience settled down, I started to demonstrate weapons. I performed the three section staff, steel whip and the spear. I then began to explain to the audience that this spear was made with the uniquely durable, strong and flexible Chinese wax wood. As I had done numerous times before, I struck the wax wood staff end onto the gym floor. It snapped in two! I was shocked and paused a moment. I then said: "And if your weapon breaks, you can use it as double weapons." As I made the last comment I started to do double figure eights with the two halves of the spear. The audience cheered at my impromptu recovery.

*

1987 Mid-Autumn Lantern Festival Demonstration

In 1986 I had a class reunion at the Mayflower of China Restaurant, a restaurant in Tukwila. It was great to see students I hadn't seen in years. Oddly one of my former students from North Bend came to me and spoke about why he had left the class. He stated that he loved the school; it was one of the best things that he had ever attended. However, when I was not around one senior student left in charge abused him and other students. This senior student would spar the less experienced students and had too much contact. After getting a five inch bruise on his chest, he stopped going to my school. I apologized for his traumatic experience. The student acknowledged that it wasn't my fault.

That senior student also had issues with loyalty and his ego. He lacked loyalty, integrity, discipline, and honor. He decided that he wanted to change from our school to Tae Kwon Do. When his close friend and classmate said that we had so much more to offer, he was cut off. The senior student said the real reason was because he wanted a black belt. It was sad because this talented student had the potential to be great, and to be a Sifu in the future.

*

I was once invited to be a "special guest" at an annual Karate organizational gathering. I was paid for my time, but I didn't understand that it was an information gathering event. I found out years later that this organization borrowed techniques from other styles to enhance their own system. My students Shawn Miller and Renee Ragaza were with me for this event.

I had the group of about 80 black belts follow me in some slow Kung-Fu movements. Though I was going slow and easy, the entire group had great difficulty trying to follow my movements. Karate people never move like Kung-Fu people, so everything was very foreign to them. Though they tried, it was just not going to happen.

Steel Whip Block

I next instructed them on our speed drill. I had all the black belts "chamber" their fists. I then instructed them that one partner would try punching at the other without telegraphing any movement. The defender would try to slap block the oncoming punch. After attempting this drill for 15 minutes, I had them turn to me. I went through the entire group and not one of them could block my punch. The only one to even touch my hand was a green belt that started before I punched

The last thing I taught this group was short distance power. I demonstrated it by placing my fist on a volunteer's chest. I then explosively extended my arm, shooting the volunteer backwards. These Karate people never saw anything like this. They tried to copy my movements, but all they achieved was medium speed pushes, that lacked power.

Adam Dow and Brandon clowning after a tournament

Shawn, Renee and me after a tournament

Their headmaster remarked at the end of the event that he truly liked the short distance power. But he was ultimately impressed with my hand speed. He stated he couldn't see my hand move and all of a sudden it was in front of their student's face. I thanked him.

*

1987 High Side Kick Rainier Playfield

In 1988 I was the AAU (Amateur Athletic Union) Chinese Martial Arts Division Regional Director for Region 12. This region covered Alaska, Inland Empire, Pacific Northwest, Pacific, Oregon and the Snake River areas. I tried to organize the Chinese martial arts school in the Seattle area. Six instructors attended the first organizational meeting. Even then I noticed that everyone was into his or her own schools. Organizing into a larger group was a futile task.

The low number of Chinese martial arts schools and the fact that most schools were not connected in any way always divided Seattle Chinese martial arts. Understanding that our Region 12 could never be similar to the successful Western Canadian Chinese Martial Arts Association, I decided to step down.

1988 classical three section staff

1988 modern knife fighting

Saving a Life
I was the Recreation Supervisor at Rainier Community Center. In 1987 I had the opportunity to save a child's life. It was approximately 10:10 p.m., on a Thursday evening. I had just sent Recreation Attendant James King home for the night. A female teenager came to the door. I thought: "Oh no, someone has a dead battery and needs a jump!" When I opened the door she stated that they needed help. I followed her to the van and there I found a co-worker, Lora Chiorah-Dye crying and screaming: "My baby!" I looked in the back seat and found her son Dumi, sitting upright, with his eyes closed and foaming at the mouth.

Spear attack cutting the back of Leroy McMillon's knee

Dumi wasn't breathing and didn't have a pulse. I grabbed the 10 year old boy and lifted him out of the van. Near the community center's front bench, I gave him a couple of back thrusts to clear anything in his throat, still no breathing. I gave him the Heimlich maneuver, but this didn't work either. I carried Dumi with my left arm as I opened up the Rainier Community Center doors. I laid him on the front door mat, and instructed his mother to call 911.

I knew I had to do CPR. I wiped his mouth and cleared it. For a brief moment I paused. I was slightly freaking out, as I was about to put my lips on a little boy! I got through that hesitation with the knowledge that this was Lora's little boy. I lifted his chin and began to do CPR. After a couple of minutes, he was still not breathing and there wasn't a pulse. I continued to do CPR and finally, I got a small movement from him. I continued to do CPR and with each of my breaths, his body started to move slightly. His eyes finally opened slightly, "glassed over" and not focusing on anything.

Medic II arrived and I gave them the details of what had happened and what I had done up to that point. They put Dumi on a stretcher and took him to the hospital. At that point I finally realized that I had just saved his life. I felt a mixture of great happiness and pride at the same time.

At the hospital, Dumi was observed and recovered well enough to go home Friday evening. He played in the Citywide Youth Basketball Championships for the 10 year old division the next day.

I was happy to have saved Dumi. The family was grateful. Though the Director at the time did mention the heroic act at a Pay Day Meeting, no commendations, or documentation occurred regarding this incident. This seemed to be just another way to "hold me down."

The Next Two Greatest Influences of My Life

The next two greatest influences of my life are my two sons, Jason and Brandon. They altered my life and changed my expectations of what things were to come.

Before having children, I was busy working, hunting and fishing with my father as well as doing martial arts. Soon after Jason was born, the hunting and fishing ceased. Working and martial arts remained constants for me.

My original thoughts were to teach my children martial arts and make sure they excelled in it. However my wife had other thoughts. She felt that they should be in mainstream sports and wanted them to do well in school sports too. I compromised my plans and agreed to her wishes.

Besides I didn't want to be an overbearing parent. I didn't want them to grow up with too much pressure to succeed. I also didn't want to force my children into daily practice. I decided that I would give them an introduction to the martial arts and leave the rest to them.

Communicating and being a strong supportive parent is what I've been. I helped them with their homework and special projects. I helped them with their mainstream sports and tried to give them confidence in their daily lives. I taught them how to drive but am not responsible for their car accidents.

2001 The Boys

They grew up always knowing that they were loved and constant support would always be there for them.

Now that they are adults, we still do activities together as often as possible. We still manage to practice Kung-Fu, play basketball, table tennis, pool, video games, workout and watch movies together.

My mother was very proud of them. She always remarked that whenever she saw them, it made her happy. She said the three of us looked like brothers. I look young because I dye my hair. I believe she also meant that she could see the love and closeness that we shared.

I have always been close to my sons. They always know that I will always support them in any way possible.

2000 Jason and Brandon with grandparents

Enlightenment of the "Why" of Taking Martial Arts

I began working for the Seattle Department of Parks and Recreation in 1984. In one of the workshops I attended a guest speaker mentioned that we had to appeal to the interests of the perspective students. Art classes must fulfill some need that the participant has. He said that some people took classes for exercise, or maybe they just wanted to be around people. Some people take classes to fulfill a fantasy that they may have of becoming a great painter or potter. He also said some people just like to learn.

I applied this to understanding why some people take martial arts classes. Some learn martial arts for cultural learning, fantasy, exercise, self defense, or comradery. This realization helped him me understand that there are many reasons why people take classes.

Rope Spear Overhand Strike

My first Kung-Fu class for Seattle Parks and Recreation was at Alki Community Center. A cute 9 year old named Jesse Perez enrolled in my Kung-Fu class. Outgoing and athletic, Jesse played indoor soccer, t-ball and basketball through the community center. During the beginning of his training, Jesse wanted to stay in the horse stance, like I wanted all students to do. Although his heart was in it and he tried as hard as he could, he couldn't handle the muscle fatigue and pain. Jesse did a great job, but just didn't have the strength and endurance of the older students. His young legs were shaking until he finally fell forward out of the stance.

Jesse cried, not from the pain, but from his perceived failure. That was when I realized that my teachings and expectations must be reduced for a larger population of "recreation" practitioners.

Acceptance By Canadian Sifus

My friendships with Canadian Sifus started in 1983. Based in Bellevue, Washington, my school competed in all the local open Karate tournaments. To see other Kung-Fu schools was rare. I met Ken Low and immediately found him to be a nice person. At one tournament Ken gave me a flyer to his West Coast CanAm Championships. I took my school up to Burnaby, B.C. and competed. We did well and liked the size of his tournament. We quickly became a fixture up there. I demonstrated at several of the West Coast CanAm Championships, as well as the Western Canadian Chinese Martial Arts Championships and Masters Exhibitions. Ken and I became very good friends. I also became friends with many of the Canadian Sifus. We went up for so many tournaments that new participants to Ken's tournaments thought I was from Canada.

Rope Spear Underhand Strike

Acceptance By Seattle Sifus

My acceptance by the Seattle based Sifus was actually based on my acceptance by the Sifus up in Canada. I knew of them prior to my involvement up in Canada. It was the numerous Canadian tournaments that the Seattle Sifus saw me at, that grew into familiarity. My acceptance by the Seattle Sifus was significant as I was viewed as the rogue, black sheep in my teens. I now had become an established as part of Seattle's traditional Kung-Fu culture.

I have had good relationships with all the Sifus in Seattle. Respect and diplomacy are always vital in any relationship.

1988 Yee Jong Kune Do Transition Into Yee Jong Pai

In 1988 I realized that I had so many different ideas and concepts, that the knowledge I needed to teach was too vast to fit into one style. I decided to create one traditional classical non-classical style and one modern combat style.

The traditional classical non-classical style became Baat Ying Baat Faat. This translates to "eight animals and eight methods." I decided this style would be comprehensive and feature the techniques of separate animal techniques as well as eight separate method techniques. The eight different animals included Tiger, Crane, snake, leopard, Dragon, Phoenix, ape and monkey. The eight different methods included soft, hard, hard power, short strikes, kicking, joint locking, continuous palm and drunken.

The modern combat style was called Yhien Dhoy Ghin Suk which simply translates into "modern warfare." The philosophy of this training is practical – no forms – just application, techniques and knowledge plus striking, grappling, joint locking, hand-held weapons and shooting weapons. Weapons would be modern or ancient, as long as they were practical and functional.

Semi-retired in 1989

Because of issues with the Seattle Department of Parks and Recreation, I stopped teaching at the community center. My classes had been raising funds for the Advisory Council that was attached to the community center that I taught at. At that time I also decided to reduce my teaching and only teach my senior students. After I promoted him to the title of Sifu, I had Michael Gibson teach classes at Delridge Community Center.

About two years later, I promoted Shawn Miller to Sifu. He taught classes at Magnolia Community Center, Queen Anne Community Center and finally at the International District/Chinatown Community Center.

The 1990s

When I went through my first divorce, my students thought I should get out socialize. My student Leroy happened to be one of the top bouncers at Papagayo's, a very popular nightclub in Bellevue, Washington. Papagayo's was the busiest nightclub in the greater Seattle area. From the time I was first married to raising my sons, I had not been to a nightclub. It felt like eons.

Leroy was working the door . My students and I went to the front of the line. Once I got inside the nightclub, I was impressed and thought: "Wow, I have been missing out!" I enjoyed myself the next couple of hours. At the end of our stay, I just innocently said: "Gee, I wouldn't mind working here." The head of security was 6 foot 5 inch Brad Anderson. He overheard my statement and asked: "Really?" I thought about it for a second and said: "Sure." My "sure" was not very assertive, more like a mix of an affirmation and a question. Brad asked if I could wait a moment.

Brad came back within a few minutes and said: "Great, you're hired!" I was totally caught off guard. I mentioned that to Brad that I was still working for the Seattle Department of Parks and Recreation at the time. He said that they could work around my primary work schedule. Brad and the manager thought that if Leroy was an asset, his Kung-Fu master would be great.

Yee Jong Pai Snake Technique with Han Saechao

Body guard and security service promotional picture

*

When 1990 Western Canadian Chinese Martial Arts Championships and Masters Exhibition arrived, I asked Shawn whether I should dress up or go casual and comfortable. Shawn thought with the long day ahead of us, casual and comfortable would be the way to go. So I dress in my black jeans, t-shirt, Reeboks and my "biker" leather jacket.

After the long drive north, we reached the tournament site. Shawn and I helped Ken Low as we usually did by judging a few divisions. At the end of the Advanced Men's Division, Hung-Ga instructor Raymond Cheung approached me. "Hi Al. Ummmmm, where's your uniform?" he questioned. I told him that I decided to dress in comfortable clothing that day. Raymond then said: "You're supposed to demo tonight!" I told him no one had asked me to demo. He stated: "You're on the poster!" Shocked, I could only say: "Really?"

Sure enough, when I checked the tournament poster, I was listed as one of the masters from the United States. I checked the tournament guide and there was my picture and bio. Certain that no one asked me to perform; I went to check with Ken Low. "Hi Ken, am I supposed to demo tonight?" No one asked me." I stated. Ken replied: "Sorry Al, we thought it would be alright for you to demo. If you didn't bring a uniform, we can substitute with someone else." At that point I asked if I could demo in my street clothes and just do self defense and application. Ken said it would be fine.

So when our turn came to demonstrate, I stepped out in a biker leather jacket and in all black. Shawn attacked me and I responded with short, quick side kicks, quick hand techniques to his head - and middle and lower body - plus joint locking techniques. I threw a couple of high side kicks to Shawn's head to demonstrate flexibility and range of foot attack. The most dramatic combination was when I quickly grabbed his lead hand and at the same time deliver a left sun fist. Then I applied an elbow lock, did a circle step and threw Shawn to the ground, still holding on to his arm. I shoulder rolled, pulled his arm outward, and I delivered right and left kicks – both above and below the outstretched arm. The crowd loved the demonstration!

*

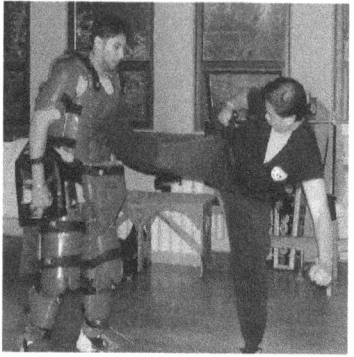  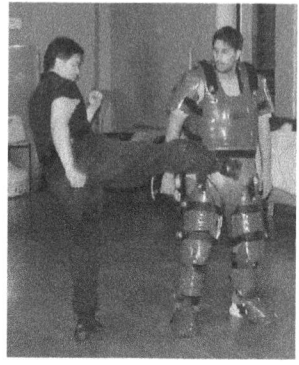

In 1991, my actress cousin Lori Tan Chinn called me up to say the upcoming Robocop 3 movie needed an Asian martial artist. I didn't have a head shot. Lori told me I needed to send one as soon as possible. I called on my best friend Larry Oliver to again help me with martial arts photos. Larry was accommodating and helpful as always. We met at Lake Sammamish State Park and took numerous martial arts pictures. Alas, I was not selected and the Robocop 3 movie came out in 1993.

1991 Robocop 3 promotional pictures

More 1991 Robocop 3 promotional pictures

First Instructional DVD

Introduction to Yee Jong Pai Kung-Fu became our first attempt to create an instructional DVD. Shawn Miller did an outstanding job shooting, coordinating and editing this project. The DVD featured me doing the principal explanations and demonstrations. Shawn Miller, Renee Ragaza-Miller, Chris Day, Dan Phan, Adam Dow and David Thanphilom also provided demonstration of techniques. Drew Hodge did a great job. However his eyes could be seen moving back and forth while reading the cue cards.

The action sequences filmed by Shawn were done very well. People loved them. However, we also received feedback that the material disseminated in this DVD was too much for most people to handle. The information was too in depth for casual martial artists and too detailed for someone not interested in theory and philosophy. It seems that most people just want more eye candy and less to think about.

From most of the feedback, we concluded that our future projects should have more action and demonstration with less explanation. This was the reverse of what we wanted to do. We wanted to actually help people understand and truly learn.

Yee Jong Pai Crane Wing Tips

The New Millennium

After hearing from members of the community that most people avoided going to the International District's Hing Hay Park because of the negative activity going on at the park, I decided to conduct a Chinese Kung-Fu Staff Class there. I thought the class would be good for the community and would give positive activity for the park.

I took the Thursday evening Kung-Fu class to Hing Hay Park one evening for a test run. Shawn and I had about eight students with us with six foot wax wood staffs. We conducted the class on the red bricks of

Hing Hay Park. As the sounds of staffs striking staffs rang out to the community, shopkeepers, customers and tourists stopped what they were doing to watch the class.

International District/Chinatown Community Center Staff Class

2005 Chinese Staff Class at Hing Hay Park

When he heard the sounds of the staffs, Thomas Spate from the Seattle Kung-Fu Club came down King Street to find out what was going on in their territory. "Oh it's just you guys!" Thomas said. We were friends. Once he found out it was us, everything was okay. We chatted for a moment and we went back to our respective business.

*

The Day of the Swordsman another special event I created to specifically highlight the "sword arts." The sword and its many variations has been used throughout by many ethnicities.

The morning of the event I was interviewed by a radio show. This interview began with the radio personality talking about the amazing sword work of the Star Wars light sabers. He then discussed our upcoming Day of the Swordsman. He promoted it as a great event and it should not be missed.

2003 World of Martial Arts 8 foot fire stick

This event was indeed spectacular and well attended. The demonstration included:

Gary Iminishi, Cascade Kendo-Kai	Kendo
Russell McCartney, Ishiyama Ryu	Japanese target cutting
Shawn Miller, Yee Jong Pai	Chinese saber and straight sword
Students of Hong Yi Jiao	Chinese straight sword
Mak Fai, Choy Li Fut	Chinese saber
Yang Family Tai Chi	Tai Chi saber and straight sword
Academia dela Spada	European sword and daggers
Jonathan Bannister, Pacific NW Budo Assoc.	Aiki-Ken and Iaido

The various schools had vendor booths and were able to promote their own school with displays and pamphlets.

Public Recreation

My first experience with public recreation was in the summer of 1974, teaching Kung-Fu at Jefferson Community Center (Seattle Parks and Recreation). I didn't teach at another public recreation program until 1983, when I taught a class at Valley Ridge Community Center (King County Parks and Recreation).

A Kung-Fu Master's Journey © 2009 Allen J. Chinn

In 1984 I was hired as a Recreation Supervisor with the Seattle Parks and Recreation. I worked at the Alki Community Center, and remember the West Seattle Herald and White Center News had an article about me and the classes that would soon be taught there.

Two years later I was transferred and began teaching at Rainier Community Center. The classes were well attended and brought in income to the Advisory Council, just as they did at Alki Community Center. The bank balance at Rainier Community Center was only $300 at the time I arrived. Kung-Fu classes did much to help purchase equipment and hire intermittent staff. While there I also created the World of Martial Arts in 1988. This was a unique fundraiser, cultural event and martial arts exhibition all rolled into one. In addition I taught a Kung-Fu program at this community center's joint programming with WSU/King County Extension Program.

After another transfer, this time to Delridge Community Center, I created a new Kung-Fu class. I taught the advanced students, but I gave Michael Gibson the day-to-day responsibility for teaching the classes, drill and basic instruction. I worked at this facility for one year.

1985 Alki Community Center

With yet another transfer, I was off to Magnolia Community Center where I had Shawn Miller teach the Kung-Fu classes. I also created "Kiddie Kung-Fu" to reach the children from ages 5 to 8 years of age. I gave my students Renee Ragaza-Miller and Maria Day the job of teaching the first class. They did a good job, but I noticed the way they were teaching was more appropriate for teaching older children. So I took over the class and added more energy in my verbal interaction. I also made the short 45 minute class fun. My students then understood how to teach this class with the younger children. I told them that this was like a "Mr. Rodger's" Kung-Fu class.

I was transferred again to Queen Anne Community Center where I would be for 11 years. Shawn Miller taught the Kung-Fu classes as well as the Middle School After School Program Kung-Fu class. Renee Ragaza-Miller his wife, taught the Kiddie Kung-Fu classes.

The World of Martial Arts exhibition resumed after a three year absence. I taught women's self defense workshops and taught at the "Chicks Play Hard" event. This event gave young girls opportunities to experience various activities and sports.

To add martial arts diversity and fitness, I hired an Aerobic Kickboxing instructor. This aerobics class had as many as 75 students in it. I also hired Chung Ying Ming to teach Chen Style Tai Chi and Blake Emery to teach Yang Style Tai Chi.

In 2004 I opened the International District/Chinatown Community Center. Shawn Miller continues to teach the Kung-Fu classes there. We added a Kung-Fu staff class at Hing Hay Park. Other martial arts programs included: Day of the Swordsman Exhibition, Kiddie Kung-Fu, Kendo Class, Teen Kung-Fu Program, Women's Self Defense and Martial Arts Fair, Women's Self Defense Workshop for IDHA, Women's Self Defense Workshop for Wing Luke Museum's Teen Program, Women's Self Defense Workshop, and the World of Martial Arts.

At the end of my career with the department, I was transferred to Miller Community Center for my remaining seven months. In October, 2008 I held the last World of Martial Arts.

1987 Seattle Aquarium Demonstration with Rainier Community Center class

2003 Women's Self Defense Workshop Krista Cabanas and Sazzy Kohli

The Difference Between Sport and Actual Combat

Sports are games. They have rules. Sports are played by athletes. The athletes may be powerful, strong, fast and coordinated. Yet in the end it is still a sport, a game. Players usually train hard and follow the rules and regulations of the specific sport.

Rules for combative sports exist for the safety of the participants. Without the rules the athletes could be severely injured, and death could occur. Even in sports deaths have taken place. People have died in boxing; point fighting and full contact mixed martial arts.

The real difference between sport martial arts and martial arts for combat is the intent – the purpose for training. The sport martial artist trains to win in the ring or the mat. The real world martial artist trains to win or survive confrontations in the street. Training may be similar, but the intent and final outcome are extremely different.

The sport martial artist trains diligently to develop powerful, fast strikes, kicks, and/or take downs. The goal may be to knock out their opponent or win by submission. The sport martial artist can use acquired knowledge in situations of self defense, and quite efficiently at times.

The combat martial artist trains for effective strikes to eyes, throat, temples, groin, joints, collar bones, spine, etc... Their training for kicks includes lightning fast kicks to knees, shins, groin, spine, etc.... or bone crushing kicks to the ribs, head or pelvis. Their grappling and joint locking training are directed towards permanent neck and joint damage, or knowledge with ability to strangle and choke opponents.

An example of sports versus combat is Wushu and Kung-Fu. Both have very intricate movements. Practitioners spend years to be accomplished in their techniques. Speed and power are developed to enhance the movements. However, Wushu practitioners do not practice striking heavy bags to make their blows more effectively injure an opponent. The Wushu practitioner does not practice sparring to develop better techniques against another opponent. They do not use weapons that are heavy or sturdy enough for a combat confrontation.

*

Years ago, when I was in Hawaii in a shopping mall. I overheard two clerks debate who was the better fighter - Jet Li or Jackie Chan. I smiled and thought to myself: "And the answer is Bruce Lee!" Though Jet Li and Jackie Chan movies are wonderfully entertaining, one must not confuse training for intent and purpose.

Jet Li was a Wushu practitioner and Jackie Chan developed his skills through Chinese Opera. Bruce Lee learned Wing Chun Kung-Fu to be an effective fighter. Though beautiful, Chinese sport/artistic based techniques can look effective and impressive, they must not be confused with real martial arts. Bruce Lee spent years of hard training to ensure his techniques were effective in the real world. He had developed many training methods and designed equipment to make his combat techniques more useful and devastating.

No one else had a steel mask made with a moveable jaw, to practice jaw breaking. No one else had huge punching bags (three times the size of a normal one) made to develop greater power and penetration. No one trained his jaws to bite an opponent more effectively. It all comes down to intent and purpose. Bruce Lee was a fighter first and an actor second.

*

Hay Hooks versus Saber

Front Kick to the Groin

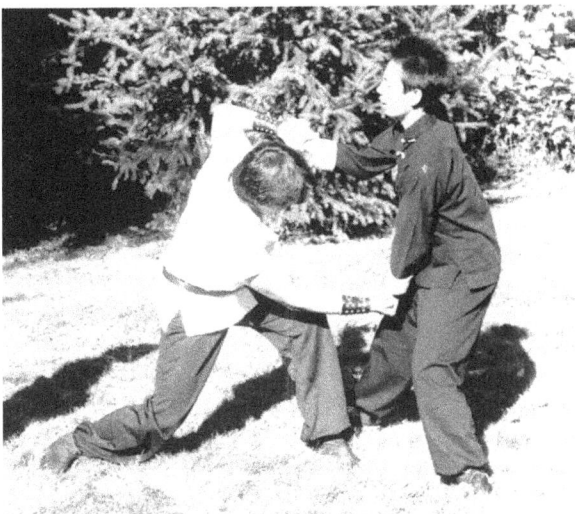
Lower Punch to the Groin

Effectiveness in actual combat has many variables to consider. One must adapt and overcome any situation in which the encounter takes place. The environment and the opponent are only some of the considerations. Does your opponent have a weapon? Is there more than one opponent? Is the area the conflict full of innocent bystanders?

Will your training be complete enough to allow you to succeed? Is your training grappling based? Or is it striking and/or kicking based? Have you been trained to use your immediate environment? Can you use improvised weapons? Are you versed in hand-held weaponry? Firearms? These are all questions one must answer if one wants to be truly ready for combat.

Yee Jong Pai Rope Spear and Saber Techniques

Iron Palm Training

From stories my father used to tell me, I had always wanted to learn Iron Palm. I knew that with my hands trained in Iron Palm, my techniques would be enhanced to a very high degree. Fast hands - able to be delivered at various angles with bone breaking impact - would be devastating.

When I was younger, I broke boards and bricks, but I wanted to be able to do it with greater ease. I studied various methods of hardening the hands and found out that there were two main methods. One was called "sacrifice training." This method has the student strike various objects to toughen and harden the fist, knife hand or palm. The other method is Iron Palm. This method has the student strike various beans, gravel and ball bearings. The striking techniques do not include using joints to impact (i.e. knuckles). Impact training using joints usually incur severe dexterity impairment. Herbal medicine is used to heal and maintain the dexterity of the hand.

In the 1980s my father and I went to Vancouver, B.C. to purchase the proper herbs to make the medicine for my Iron Palm training. After going to a few Chinese herb shops, we had the necessary ingredients to make the medicine. We brought them back to Seattle, cooked the herbs and stored the ingredients in a large clay pot.

I tried to use the medicine to train with but found it very difficult to be able to train the required routine of three times a day. I was working and could not interrupt my workday to ensure I got in the afternoon session. Having my hands immersed in toxic medicine, would make it difficult to take care of two very busy young boys. Finally, there was a peculiar odor on my hands that lasted a while.

Knowing this I decided that I could not do the Iron Palm training. I realized I could not follow the old world training schedule to be successful. I then thought of a book I had read on the subject. One Tai Chi master asked an Iron Palm expert to attack him with the two hands that were deadly weapons. The Iron Palm expert could not touch the Tai Chi master. I then believed that because of my work, my children and other commitments of our modern society, I could not train in Iron Palm. I decided that increasing my knowledge and ability would be more beneficial for me than having hands of steel.

Firearms?

Throughout my years in martial arts, I have always been approached by people who asked me: "What would you do if I had a gun?" My philosophy is that firearms are a natural extension of Kung-Fu. Throughout history there have been many throwing and shooting weapons in Chinese martial arts. Dart guns, bow and arrows, hand held cannons and others have been used in conflicts in China.

The ancient Chinese Night Walkers (or Vagabonds) were the supposed forerunners of Japanese Ninjitsu. At beginning of the 1900s, there was the modern version of these original covert ops martial artists. They dressed in all black to blend in with the shadows. They had large balloon leg pants, so they could relieve themselves without having to drop their pants. The pant legs were tied and gathered at the shins during combat. They carried a saber, throwing weapons and an 1896 Broom Handle Mauser pistol.

Chinese Night Walker

The 7.63x25mm (30 Mauser) pistol was used once the covert part of the operation was compromised. Though loud, it was a way to return firepower in those days. As a 10 shot pistol, it fired an 86 grain bullet at a velocity of 1,400 feet per second. This was the most modern and most powerful handgun of its time.

Firearms were a natural progression of combat oriented martial artists. Not including firearms makes no sense in the context of fully understanding what is true martial arts. Martial arts literally translates to "war art." The word "modern," relates to the present and recent time.

If we look historically at many hand held weapons, we find a common factor. Sword, knives, arrows and other weapons have been effective by having a little piece of metal penetrate the body. A little piece of metal is a little piece of metal whether it is a blade, arrowhead, pointed steel rod or a bullet.

1987 Colt CAR 9mm   **Instructing 15 year old Jason with S&W Model 66 357 Magnum**

My own history with firearms started from training with my father. My introduction to shooting was about the same time I started learning Kung-Fu. My father was an avid hunter. He taught me how to shoot a rifle and a shotgun. My interests in this area lead me to become very knowledgeable in firearms and related subjects. I have competed in trap shooting, turkey shoots and some combat oriented matches. I've owned and used sporting, hunting and combat firearms. I have even owned and used black powder muzzleloaders as well as cap and ball revolvers. I reloaded my own ammunition for shotguns, handguns and rifles. I also worked in the firearms industry for a number of years.

*

About 1988, several of my Canadian Sifu friends came down to participate in shooting with me. We went out Highway 18. Back in those days there was a bunch of land next to the freeway that was opened for the public to shoot at. I took everyone in my big Chevy Nomad RV van. The Canadian Sifus took to shooting with energy and excitement. Ken, Neil, Roger and Ernie absolutely loved it. They got to shoot combat shotguns, AR-15s, HK 91s, a M-11, Browning Hi Power, Colt 1911, and a Sig Sauer 226.

They were in heaven! Neil thanked me for making his "dreams come true!" They didn't have chances to target shoot, or plink out in the woods in Canada. To shoot exotic firearms and in rapid fire, was truly special for them.

At the next couple of tournaments here in Washington and up in Canada, my other instructor friends heard about the great shooting expedition and indicated that they wanted to do so also. Even Roger Tung approached me at a Steve Curran's tournament and stated he would like to go out and shoot with me.

Firearms are an intriguing fascination. Some of the world's most talented martial artists desire to learn and use firearms.

A Kung-Fu Master's Journey © 2009 Allen J. Chinn

Canadian Sifus happy and ready for target practice

Shooting off of Highway 18

Masters and Martial Arts Friends

Over the years I made many martial arts friends. Many friendships have been for over twenty years. Here are a few of my close friends.

Ken Low

I met Ken during the early 1980s. We became friends attending the same tournaments. I started attending his West Coast Can-Am Championships annually. He has a diverse martial arts background, holding a black belt in Tae Kwon Do, instructor in My Jong Law Horn Kung-Fu and Wushu. He is also knowledgeable in Choy Li Fut, Dragon Sign, Bak Mei and Hung-Ga Kung-Fu.

He was the Western Canadian Chinese Martial Arts Association's President for many years. Ken has always been a great friend and I have enjoyed our friendship for the last 25 years.

I was judging at one of Ken's West Coast CanAm Championships. One Kung-Fu instructor was upset with the mediocre score that he had received from me. He was venting to Ken about me and said, "Who does that guy think he is?" My friend Ken simply replied, "I wouldn't mess with him up close, or out to 600 yards!" The disgruntle Kung-Fu instructor was puzzled by that answer, but later found out more about me through the various instructors.

*

Neil Chan

Neil had been part of a group of Canadian Kung-Fu competitors I met at Jerry Gould's tournaments in the early 1980s. We became close friends and since our last names were the same, we started calling each other cousin or "cuz" for short.

His skill in Dragon Sign Kung-Fu and Bak Mei Kung-Fu is great. Neil also cross trained in Karate, Tae

Sifus Ken Low and Allen Chinn **Sifus Neil Chan and Allen Chinn**

Kwon Do and grappling. He was the Chief Director of the West Coast Can-Am for numerous years. He was rated Top 15 in Canada and was NBL (National Black Belt League) rated number five in Heavyweight sparring division in 2000, for the Pacific Northwest Region. He was also the founder of the West Coast Warrior Team and head coach.

We used to joke that it would be cool to be instructors for a rich nobleman in Saudi Arabia. We could teach on the weekdays and fly home for the weekends. What dreams we had!

*

Sid Woodcock

My dear friend and former boss, I met Sid in 1982. I worked for Detonics Manufacturing as Technical Representative in Marketing when he was the President of the company. We hit it off right away at my interview. We discovered that we had a lot in common, especially a firearms and martial arts background.

Sid has an extensive background in Aiki-Jujitsu. He holds a black belt from the Kodokan in Japan. He also studied Shaolin Kung-Fu for several years while behind enemy lines during World War II. He was also a Karateka.

Grandmaster Woodcock's Accomplishments:
- Grandmaster, 3rd Style Shaolin Kung-Fu
- 8th Degree Black Belt in Shinobi
- Instructor, U.S. Army Special Forces, Ft. Bragg
- Instructor, U.S. Navy Seal Teams
- Consultant, U.S. Department of Defense
- Consultant, Federal Bureau of Investigation
- Consultant, Central Intelligence Agency
- Consultant, U.S. Secret Service
- Director and Federal Liaison for Special Warfare, in the areas of counter terrorist training.

I remember one time the sales manager at Detonics gave me some trouble when I had a hard time following his poor directions. Sid came over to me and stated, "Don't worry about him. We both know we can out-shoot him, outfight him, and out f**k him!" I smiled and Sid got me to be less stressed about the incompetent sales manager.

*

Kregg Jorgenson

Kregg is an amazing friend that I met in the late 1980s. I turns out that I actually met Kregg in 1983 at the Seattle Open. He reminded me that I gave him a good score on his Karate Bo kata. It is a small world. Years later he reminded me that he was the person that, at the conclusion of my demonstration at my Factoria Square Mall, asked a very simple question: "What would you do if I pulled out my gun?" My response was: "I'd run around the corner and then shoot you with my pistol!" Kregg told me he was always impressed with that answer.

Years later I found out that one of my favorite martial arts stories "When Two Tigers Meet," was written for a martial arts magazine by none other than Kregg. This story was a about a young martial artist who went to a Karate school and wanted to spar with the instructor. He highlighted an old Chinese saying: "When two tigers meet, one will be dead and the other will be mauled." It was indeed a memorable and profound story.

When I was teaching Leroy McMillon, he told me a couple of times that his former Karate instructor wanted to do a magazine article on me. I thought "Yeah, right."

Finally about 1987, Kregg interviewed me with questions over the phone. We hit it off immediately. When Kregg started the interviewing process, we talked for a couple of hours. He was impressed with my knowledge and "real world" practicality for self defense and combat. Since then Kregg has written numerous magazine articles about me in Inside Kung-Fu, Black Belt, Karate-Kung-Fu Illustrated, and Tae Kwon Do Times.

Kregg has a diverse martial arts background. He has studied Karate, Tae Kwon Do, Arnis, Kung-Fu, Arrestling, Ju Jitsu and was almost 50 years old when he took up Judo. Though Kregg was a 3rd degree black belt in Japanese Karate, he wanted to learn different arts. That is when he became a student of mine. Kregg was unlike any student I had or have had since. He enjoyed hard workouts. Whenever I commanded drills or exercises, Kregg had a positive and energetic attitude about doing them. His attitude was "Oh boy, I get to do this!" Kregg was intelligent and talented. He learned quickly and absorbed information like a sponge.

After studying Kung-Fu with me, Kregg sent his Karate organization into a tail spin. They could not understand why he was learning Kung-Fu as the head of their organization. They didn't understand Kregg. They didn't know that he possessed an undying desire to learn and was not only a great teacher, but still a great student. He was indeed a rare jewel!

As Kregg learned more from me, he understood that I knew quite a bit. He stated that no one would take me seriously. I was too young, and I was not from China. He said we could make lots of money if we grayed my hair, posed as an immigrant from China and pretended to speak no English. Kregg said all I had to do was whisper in his ear, and he would say: "Grandmaster Chinn said…" Kregg had a great sense of humor.

Kregg noted that there were very few people with my abilities. Few masters were as gifted in so many facets of the martial arts. Some masters were gifted in one area such as striking, kicking, joint locking or weaponry. He had never met anyone that was highly skilled in all those areas as well as with modern weaponry. He appreciated my pragmatic approach to what works and what doesn't.

Today Kregg has a 6th degree black belt in Japanese Karate. He was a highly decorated soldier with the Army, a Vietnam Veteran, writer for the Army and a prolific freelance writer. He is currently a Supervisor with U.S. Customs and is a published author of several books.

1988 Kregg Jorgenson and Binky Almanza   **1997 brother Mike and me**

Mike Shintaku

I was at Bob Hill's Butokukan Karate Tournament in 1983 when this big Japanese guy walked into the gym. He had his sunglasses and flip flops on. My first impression: here is this cool guy from either Hawaii or California. Later I found out he was from California. Mike is a very talented martial artist and posses a black belt in Shito-Ryu Karate and is a 7th dan in Tang Soo Do.

We became friends as we were always bumping into each other at the local tournaments. At one tournament Wayne Underwood said that Mike and I looked like brothers. I didn't think so. I thought Wayne just thought all Asian guys looked alike. I mentioned it to Mike and he asked his wife Melanie: "Do we look like brothers?" Melanie looked at both our faces and said: " Yes, you two could pass for brothers." I was quite surprised, but that is how Mike became my bro and Melanie my sis.

*

Michael Bowser

I met Michael at the Jerry Gould tournaments in the early 1980s. He was a talented black belt and always competed in those tournaments. I didn't realize that I knew Michael's younger brothers in high school. Famous for his Sanchin Kata and his Oar Kata, Michael just considers himself a student of Shorin-ryu (Shaolin style), and follows the Chinese approach of impact techniques that whip. He does not view his many years as a 4th degree black belt, anymore than just time put in. Michael has always been very talented, knowledgeable and humble.

*

Sensei Mike Bowser and Okinawan Oar   **Sensei Jeanne Misha Carter**

Jeanne Carter

Seeing Jeanne Misha Carter compete was a joy. She used to compete in hand and weapons forms and fighting. She was always a great competitor and very successful too. Her katas were always beautiful and precise. A 4th degree black belt in Shito-Ryu Karate, she also teaches Cardio Kickboxing. She is as beautiful on the inside, as she is on the outside.

*

The World of Martial Arts

I started the first World of Martial Arts in 1988. As a teenager, I remembered reading about a martial arts exhibition performed in New York. I liked the name and that is how I came to name this event of diverse martial arts and culture: the World of Martial Arts.

The World of Martial Arts came into existence to enlighten the citizens of Seattle about the world's wonderful, ethnically diverse martial arts. This event featured local masters and experts, volunteer to demonstrate their prowess in ancient martial arts.

The World of Martial Arts also brought together diverse parts of the martial arts community that had never partnered collectively. The masters and experts of the many disciplines almost never met. Sometimes it was because the styles were profoundly different. Other times it was that the masters had previously chosen to be closed off from other schools.

In April 16, 1988 was the first time the diverse martial arts in the greater Seattle area came together for a community center fundraiser. This event showed diverse cultural martial arts from far off lands at its first site, the Rainier Community Center gym. I solicited a variety of masters and experts to participate. Some came to assist with the community center in mind while some took part to promote themselves and their school.

2002 World of Martial Arts the only time Brandon and Jason performed on stage with me

There were no other events that brought together martial arts experts and masters from punch-kick, grappling, joint locking, and traditional weapon arts. The classical martial arts that were represented and the rich ethnic diversity of the experts and masters was truly representative of this multi-cultural community and region. I felt truly proud of this special event.

The World of Martial Arts has been truly an inclusive multi-cultural event. A few veteran instructors and masters assist every year and bring not only support for this event, but also support for the entire martial arts community.

Great clay, or a Great Potter?

Once I had an interesting conversation with my top disciple Shawn Miller. The discussion centered on which was more important: a great student, or a great style. A great style could propel a good student to heights that could never be achieved otherwise. A great student would have the dedication to achieve a high level regardless of the style.

I started to use a metaphor involving great clay or a great potter. Which is more important?

A great potter is needed to make a masterpiece. Without the skill of the potter the clay project would be less than perfection. However, great clay is needed to make a great vase. A master potter cannot make a masterpiece without quality clay. Inferior clay with lumps and debris cannot be used to make a masterpiece.

So there is a need for both. A balance is very important. However the quality of the clay is the fundamental ingredient for success. A master potter needs quality clay to create a masterpiece.

The Kung-Fu Anti-Christ

The normal precept of martial arts is to practice, practice, practice!!! When I was young, I tried to practice three hours a day. As I got older, I didn't have that much time. No one does. Life takes over. More work, a significant other, children, everything that goes with a home, school and the children's activities, etc... So training and practicing became things of the past. I noticed the first thing to go was my legs. Although I had no more strong stances, but I could still do my six foot-plus high side kicks. This lasted until my mid-40s.

The last couple of years my side kick has dropped to about five feet high. My round house kicks have also dropped to five feet high. With lots of stretching, I can get another 6 inches. I can still kick high with front kicks and crescent kicks. Surprisingly, I maintained my hand speed, power and joint locking abilities. For many years (the last 20) I haven't truly practiced. Students and my instructor friends are always amazed that I can still do all this without practice.

So for the last 15 years or so I've told people I'm the Anti-Christ! I don't train or practice, but I'm still able to perform techniques at a high level. Students, however, should practice as often as they can. I attribute my high level of skill and retention to those numerous 3 to 4 hour practices I did when I was young.

Non-Typical Kung-Fu Master

There seemed to be a paradox whenever people would ask about my expertise in the martial arts. This would usually take place after they found out I was a firearms expert as well. Most people thought that both skills and philosophies were contrary to each other. I explained that they were complimentary, stating: "Firearms are just another tool in self defense, combat and warfare."

*

When John Caston first joined us at the Bellevue Kung-Fu Club, he only had a Ninjitsu uniform. So he wore that and Ninjitsu tabis until he could afford the new Kung-Fu uniform. So, he was nicknamed "Ninja John." John was also a black belt in Tae Kwon Do. John was interested in doing bodyguard work. He had attended classes at ESI (Executive Security International) in Colorado.

In 1988 John arranged for me to teach a workshop out in Baring, Washington, an out of the way place near Index, Washington, was in Snohomish County. I taught archery, handguns, rifles, shotguns, knife fighting and hand-to-hand combat. His friends paid me to travel to this remote site.

On that sunny Saturday afternoon my students and I finally arrived. All of John's friends waiting there for us. I stepped out of my van wearing sunglasses, a muscle shirt, and shorts. I was eating Cheetos and drinking a Diet Coke. They looked shocked because I did not look like anything they had expected.

Two Hand Straight Sword versus Nine Ring Horse Chopper

I began by demonstrating combat applications with handguns, assault rifles and combat shotguns. The students were impressed with the various firearms and their configurations. After live firing at various targets and demonstrating rapid fire exercises, I switched to archery. The archery was demonstrated on a compound bow, with sights and a mechanical release. I explained that this modern version of an ancient weapon could be as accurate as a handgun and was a silent self defense tool.

We took a break and my students were having fun in the cold river. The sand was beautiful and had tiny bits of shiny material in it. Leroy McMillon and Mike Gibson were standing on large river rocks (boulders actually) and were knife fighting with the wooden tantos that John's friend Jay brought to the workshop. Jay was a violin maker and had crafted some beautiful oak knives the same size and shape of the Cold Steel Tanto.

Mike and Leroy were having fun while trying to stay out of the freezing water of the river. The were evenly matched. It was a "tie" as the defense-minded Leroy and the offense-minded Mike canceled each other out. As everyone gathered again for instruction, a tall 6'3" friend of John's named Dale wanted in on the action of sparring with the wooden knives. I told him that my students did not spar with people from outside the class. Dale said: "Come on I'll be okay. I made it through Vietnam and I'm still in one piece."

Dale kept egging us on and wanted to spar with the oak knives. All my students looked at me. They didn't want to refuse the apparent challenge, but knew our policy about sparring outsiders. Dale continued to dare our school into sparring. "Not one of you are going to spar with me?" he said. Then Leroy looked at me and reluctantly agreed to spar with Dale.

As they both saluted each other, both men got ready for the contest. Leroy was a good defensive, counter fighter. Dale on the other hand, had bizarre unorthodox techniques. He would hold the knife high up, switch hands behind his back, did crazy "goose steps" with a lot of fake attacks. This threw Leroy off guard, and Dale scored several "stabs" on Leroy. They ended their match and Leroy had surprisingly lost.

Dale was now "pumped" and became more boastful and wanted another match. He became more obnoxious and continued to badger us. I was getting irritated and just as I was about to take him, Mike said he would spar with him. Mike was 16 years of age, a talented soft spoken student.

Both participants got ready and saluted each other. Suddenly, Mike stepped forward and unleashed a quick, single knuckle strike, but with the knife tip. The tip of the oak knife struck Dale squarely on his sternum. It was so fast and aggressive that it shocked Dale. Dale was unsuccessful with the unorthodox movements that had worked for him previously. He was not able to get reactions from a defensive fighter to create openings. He instead, became the target of a barrage of aggressive attacks from Mike.

Beaten easily by our talented teenager, Dale was silenced. No longer boastful and obnoxious, he followed the class format, became obedient and was respectful of the directions that were given. The rest of the workshop went smoothly. The knife fighting drills and hand-to-hand combat was well received.

*

Double Sickles versus four foot staff

Arm Lock with Noel Lakey

People I Had Promoted to Sifu Status

My standards are very high. In 45 years of martial arts experience, I have only promoted five individuals to the title of Sifu. Michael Gibson, Leroy McMillon, Shawn Miller, Rich Brady and Renee Ragaza-Miller are on this very short list. Only Michael Gibson, Shawn Miller, and Renee Ragaza-Miller are still practicing and teaching.

To be promoted to Sifu, a student must be able to physically perform the techniques taught to them at a high level. Students that attain a level of "black belt equivalent" are not considered to to be Sifus. More important yet, they must possess the correct attitude and spirit. They must follow my teachings, live the philosophies and teach in a benevolent way.

Respect. Discipline. Perseverance. Dedication. Desire. Honor. Integrity. Loyalty. All students must follow these words, the Sifu must always be the highest example of these imperatives. The Sifu must always consider what is best for the organization and his, or her masters. I consider the organization to be our family structure. One must never let the masters and the organization down.

Sifu Michael Gibson

Michael Gibson

In 1983 Michael started training with me when he was 13 years old. He and his friend, Jason Tetlow, came to my school to enroll. Michael was a smaller 13 year old and Jason was rather tall for his age. They both worked hard to keep up with the grueling class. With their new uniforms soaked with sweat, they both left their first day of class totally exhausted. I thought Jason did well enough, but I wasn't sure Michael would return. To my surprise Jason was the "one day student" and Michael had the bigger heart.

Michael continued to work hard and at the end of one year, his first form (Jong Hop Kune) looked great. From there he started to learn faster and faster. He was a sponge and soaked up all the techniques and forms quite easily.

Michael was the first student I had promoted to the title of Sifu. He has taught for me at various schools throughout the years.

Michael continues training hard. Over the years has increased his power and strength. He convincingly uses a combination of strength, power, speed and finesse, when sparring full contact with our younger instructors.

Sifu Shawn Miller

Shawn Miller

Shawn started training with me about 20 years ago. He had practiced for about 10 years prior to meeting me. He was an eager student and learned everything very easily. Of all my students throughout the years, Shawn had learned the most from me.

He too was a sponge for knowledge and carefully videotaped each form. His record keeping of the forms was vital reference material.

Shawn represented our style at various tournaments in Canada, the Pacific Northwest and San Francisco. Choy Li Fut Sifu Fred Spencer saw me demonstrate at the 1991 Western Canadian Chinese Martial Arts Championships and Masters Exhibition. Afterwards he invited me to go to San Francisco to demonstrate at his 1991 U.S. Open Kung-Fu Championships. I respectfully declined (I was never much of a traveler and I had children to take care of), but suggested Shawn could take my place. Shawn did an outstanding performance for Sifu Spencer.

For years I have named Shawn as the Chief Instructor of our style. I have been semi-retired from teaching, only teaching our senior students, workshops and teen classes.

Sifu Renee Ragaza-Miller

Renee Ragaza-Miller

Renee trained with me, first learning the basic Jong Hop Kune and Yao Kune forms. I decided that with her body type, I would teach her a special style. I created Luk Ying Duin Dah (Six Animal Short Strikes) specifically for her. This style uses fast, fluid animal movements of the tiger, leopard, crane, dragon, snake and phoenix.

Whenever Renee demonstrated or competed, women would come up to her and complement her on her technique.

*

I have two senior students who are at the "black belt level" and are our first level instructors. They have always trained hard and one day will be promoted to Sifu status. David Thanphilom and Adam Dow will continue to work towards reaching the title of Sifu.

Ranking

In most traditional Chinese martial arts schools there is no ranking. The Sifu is the father figure. Senior students are viewed as older brothers and sisters. All the students, assistant instructors, and the head instructor know the skill level of each other. Skill is skill. No matter how long you've been in the school, or your perceived rank, everyone knows whether you're better or worse than them.

With this in mind I never thought about a ranking system. It was the purpose of all students to train hard and obtain better skills to become more proficient in their Kung-Fu techniques.

Kregg Jorgensen had suggested a ranking system since the late 1980s. Since Kregg was a Japanese stylist, he was quite familiar with working in a system that had ranking and testing. Kregg also tried to help me modify my system in order to be more financially feasible.

Kregg explained to me that all the Japanese and Korean styles had ranking, and the instructors and organizations had a revenue stream from testing fees. He also pointed out that many of the students taking martial arts value their accomplishments when it is certified by a piece of paper. The American mind values that piece of paper. That is why certificates and diplomas mean so much to those people.

We went round and round on the subject in the late 1980s and a second time in the late 1990s. Nothing ever became a ranking system for Yee Jong Pai Kung-Fu.

Why I Used the Title of Grandmaster

In the 1980s my students started to become heavily involved with tournaments, I saw a disparity in skill levels and in ranking. Some martial artists were very skilled and others were not. I could see this in the students and also among the instructors.

Prior to opening the Bellevue Kung-Fu Club, I always had my students just call me "Allen." Once I had a formal school, I taught my students to call me "Sifu." I did this to increase the respect level of the students and to create a better atmosphere for discipline and organization.

My students became quite skilled and once a few were promoted to the title of Sifu, I became the next higher level. I was the Sifu of the new student's Sifu. This was much like the father, becoming the grandfather, or the grandfather becoming the great-grandfather. At that point I could have used the title of Grandmaster (Si-Gung) but didn't do so.

It wasn't until a few students of disreputable instructors and schools made a hugely negative impression on me. These schools and instructors were shameless and were teaching less than quality Karate and passed it off as Kung-Fu. These schools scammed unknowing students into paying huge monthly tuitions. They also "worked" them by having them pay extra funds for their "inner circle" training.

Sometimes students of these shams would see the truth and become very angry with the school. Others would defend their schools because they didn't know any better. Sometimes people refuse to admit to themselves that they had been "taken."

Furthermore, the figureheads of their organizations often claimed to Grandmaster of this, or that. I had finally had it with these scammers that didn't know the history of Kung-Fu or the techniques of Kung-Fu. I felt these people had no honor or integrity. They never met other Sifus, were never at tournaments and would not attend exhibitions. These people were the latest version of the 1970s Kung-Fu sham artists that had their students meet them at a different park each week. They changed to having schools only so they could take people for more money.

It was then that I decided to use the title of Grandmaster. In Chinese Kung-Fu circles, when introducing instructors, they are usually referred to as Sifu. Grandmaster (Si-Gung), or Great Grandmaster (Dai Si-Gung) was used internally within the Kung-Fu school, or organization. Soon other Sifus started to use the title of Grandmaster, likely because of the American influence and the fact that some actual martial arts styles called their high level instructors Grandmaster, Supreme Grandmaster and other exotic titles.

Eight Words a Martial Artist Should Live By

Respect. Discipline. Perseverance. Dedication. Desire. Honor. Integrity. Loyalty.

These words are vital for a martial artist to live by. Better yet, all people should live by these words. Relationships of all kinds would improve dramatically.

I have been blessed to have students who understand these words and follow them. And yet I have also been cursed to have students who were the total opposite. These individuals are harmful to any possible harmony in organizations, relationships and work environments.

Quality Student / Quality Person

I cannot overemphasize the importance of a quality student. This person learns and trains with enthusiasm. They develop their skills rapidly because of their effort and devotion.

The quality student is moral and just in all his or her interactions. They do not take advantage of others, nor do they find pleasure in hurting others emotionally or physically. They do not take pleasure in making fun of others. They are mature in their behavior.

I always felt positive energy when teaching someone who is moral, honorable and honest. After many years I still fondly remember my best students. By best I mean the best skill and techniques, but also the best quality people.

On the contrary, teaching individuals who have no integrity, honor or morality is a waste of time. These people take advantage of any situation and are innately selfish. These people also leave a lasting impression on me, but only in a negative way. I have no respect for these individuals.

*

I can't remember when the article was written, but an Inside Kung-Fu article highlighted Eagle Claw Master Shum Leong. He said that in the old days a good master was hard to find. He felt today, it is a good student who is hard to find. I believe that both a good master and a good student are hard to find.

Bigotry and Prejudice I Have Endured

There are wonderfully diverse people that understand the color of one's skin is a non-issue. Because one is different (race, gender, religion, ideology, interests, income level, education level, etc), differences should be celebrated. Unfortunately, there are still people who feel if you are different, you are not as good as they are. Because you are different, you are not given the same opportunities. Because you are different, you are treated with negative consideration and treated poorly.

Fear and ignorance are the cornerstones of bigotry and prejudice. Being non-white certainly has been a stumbling block because of the bigoted minority

As an American born Chinese there have also been issues with my inability to speak fluent Chinese. Most people understand, but occasionally I have had some Chinese immigrants that looked down on me for not being able to speak Chinese. Cantonese, Mandarin or Toisonese? You just can't please everyone.

I've dated women who were not of Asian descent. I have always felt people were just people. So it was funny to hear: "You're the first Asian person I've gone out with." It sounded like Asians were so very different. I usually responded with: "Our lips taste the same as anyone else's."

Being a martial artist many people use stereotype visions to reinforce their notion that martial artists are violent people. I think they get their understanding from watching too many B grade movies. They probably never researched what real martial arts are all about, so they don't know.

Up until my mid-twenties I was viewed negatively by many of the established Chinese martial arts schools. I was considered a black sheep martial artist that made up his Kung-Fu. Even my father once called my Kung-Fu "chop suey" - referring to it as a mixture of many different ingredients. Once the established martial arts entities saw what my style was actually about, I was embraced and became part of that community.

Being a gun person has also been an issue at times. Anti-gun people are just like any other group who are not open minded. They believe that their thoughts are the only valid side to an issue. Again, I've been lumped into violent behavior, yet I have no violent offenses nor a police record. Amazing that people get their information and biased reasoning from watching too much television or movies and think that is reality.

Even in gun circles there still is a lack of open mindedness. Many people that are hunters or sports competitors cannot understand why "assault rifles" should even be permitted. They don't understand that they're purchased and owned for fun and recreation. They only shoot one shot per pull of the trigger, just like their hunting, or competitive firearms. I have owned assault rifles that I use for recreational target shooting. Again, I have no police record and have never "assaulted" anyone with one of these assault rifles.

Just because of outward appearances, people assume (making an ass of you and me). I have a couple of sports cars, but I don't speed. My driving record is very clean. On my Dodge Stealth I added an aluminum duo spoiler. The car already had a factory spoiler, but I wanted to add this one to it also. Seeing this car people would assume that I'm a young street racer. I have been followed by squad cars, but once they ran my plates, they knew that I was an old man (usually older than the officer checking on me) and my record was clean.

When I had a Federal Firearms License I used to do business with Southern Ohio Guns. My business license and FFL had the name of Yee Jong Kune Do. I remember one day I called to place an order. The salesperson asked what the FFL name was. I spelled it for her: Yee Jong Kune Do. She found it and tried to pronounce it: Yee Jong Kunie Du? I pronounced it correctly for her and she asked what that was. I told her it was the name of my Chinese martial arts style. She then asked: "Are you Chinese?" I replied yes, and then she stated: "You don't sound Chinese."

I also did business with a firm called Bill Hicks and Company Ltd. I was trying to find a scope mount for a Chinese made Polytech M-14 rifle. The salesperson said: "We don't carry scope mounts for Chink rifles. I wrote a complaint letter and stopped doing business with this company.

When I was managing the gun shop at Auburn Sports and Marine, I ran several combat oriented tournaments to promote the store. One combat pistol competitor seemed to be supportive of my work and the tournaments. I thought he was a decent person. I was told later that he was a bigot. He was a Vietnam War veteran and was prejudice against Asian people. I originally felt: "No not this person." I have had numerous friends that were veterans from the Vietnam War and had no prejudice against people of any ethnicities. But I was told again by one of my customers and friend, that he was nice to my face, but called me a "gook" behind my back.

One of my sons as a teenager once said: "We're the best at martial arts because we're Asian." I quickly asked who my best student was and he replied: "Shawn." I then pointed out that Shawn was Black. I said it was fine to be proud of what you are. But it is what you do that makes you the best, not your race.

*

In my early twenties when I was dating my future wife, she had a coworker who was supposed to be a reincarnated Tibetan prince. He did suffer from delusions of grandeur. At first he seemed friendly but then his true colors came out. He was rude and tried to antagonize me. He made ignorant remarks that Chinese (Cantonese, or Mandarin) should all be the same. Maybe he didn't like Chinese because of China-Tibet relations.

He didn't know of my martial arts background, but he was afraid of another martial artist we both knew. He knew that I was in the firearms industry, and because of my easy going nature, decided I would be an easy target for him.

This guy even walked in front of me, stepping on my feet when I was in a conversation with another person. He did not bat an eye, or apologize for the action, and I knew that this guy was a total jerk. I wanted to tell this guy off, but Connie would not permit me to.

One day while I was waiting for Connie at her office, this person knew I had to wait for her meeting to be completed. He said: "Great! Now we can debate gun control." The last thing I wanted to do was to have more interaction with this pompous fool. He was studying to be an attorney and went on the offensive immediately. "Why do you feel you have to carry a gun?" he asked. I replied: "Because the police cannot be everywhere every minute of the day. I believe we need to be able to protect ourselves." He attacked with: "So you're saying police can't do their job." I responded with: "No that is not what I said. If someone were attacking you right now would the police be able to protect you? No, you would have to rely on yourself." He then rapid fired questions at me without giving me a second to respond to any of them.

Like a good martial artist, I then changed my tactic and said: "You know people don't like you." This blew him out of the water. No longer was he trying to ramrod his thoughts on anti-gun issues to me and prove he was better than me in some fashion. Now he tried to justify why people liked him. I thought this was quite funny.

Once had a meeting with the Superintendent of the Parks and Recreation Department. He was not even in our Department for a year, but had been hired by the Mayor to be the department head. When I arrived for my 1:00 p.m. meeting with the Superintendent that day, I heard an acquaintance, a patrol sergeant I knew from the Chinatown area, tell the receptionist that he was supposed to meet with the Superintendent at the same time. As the officer walked by me, we greeted each other and he asked what I was doing there. I said: "I just have a meeting here." He left, but I noticed another patrolman was sitting in front of the building the entire time the meeting had taken place.

"Does the Superintendent actually have police officers waiting outside the building just in case something happened with me? Unreal!" I shook my head and laughed to myself. True, I was a martial artist and firearms hobbyist, but I did not have a police record or any propensity for violence. There was never any history or evidence of this. This situation was a prime example of fear and ignorance manifested into bigotry and prejudice at the highest level of a department. I wondered why he wasn't also afraid of the police officers.

Training Family Members

Years ago Connie had admitted that Kung-Fu was more practical than her beloved ballet. She started taking classes at the Kent school and attended a few sessions. Connie and my friend's wife Carol were doing drills together in class one day. We switched from striking and blocking drills to joint locking. After I gave instructions, Connie refused to grab Carol's arm. I explained that she had to. She still refused. I tried to assure her that it wasn't a big deal, but she still refused to cooperate with the partner joint locking drill. I was put in an awkward position, as my directive was not followed. Even the instructor's wife must conform to directions, just like any other student. Favoritism was not permitted. That was the last class she ever attended.

Uncle Joe with Kim, Kay and Kai in front of Chinn's Electric   **Sifu Kay Chinn**

While I was at Rainier Community Center my cousin Kay trained with me for about a year or so. When I was transferred, he started training under Mak Fai. Years went by. When I started to work in the International District. I was in contact with him again. He happened to be managing the building where the new community center was located in. Small world indeed. Kay demonstrated for me at the World of Martial Arts. He works out with my students at the International District/Chinatown Community Center.

1983 Jim Jorgensen helping with demo at Factoria Square Mall

My brother-in-law Jim Jorgensen took classes from me at the Bellevue Kung-Fu Club in 1983. He hadn't a great deal of physical exercise for a while, so Kung-Fu was a new challenge. But he did well and even helped with a demonstration at Factoria Square Mall. One day he was working out with Bruce Friedman. Jim threw kicks at Bruce and Bruce was just quick enough to catch them. But as Bruce held Jim's leg, Jim jumped and threw speedy hook kick at Bruce's head. It barely missed Bruce's head. This sequence happened two more times.

The third time was not a happy event for Jim. On this attempt, he fell on his elbow. This impact with the floor popped his shoulder out of joint. He was in such pain we called 911. Soon an Aide car was on the scene. They took Jim to Overlake Hospital and reinserted the ball of the arm into the socket.

*

My sons Jason and Brandon as well as my nephews Adam and Patrick, used to train with me at our special Sunday class. Invited a few other students also. It was a great class. We did sword and staff work, as well as technique development and sparring. I held the class on the front lawn, so we got quite a few stares from the neighborhood.

One day I brought out a Samurai sword. It was an inexpensive stainless steel one. I showed the students what I wanted done by taking the sword and started chopping a large bush in the front yard. I continued to round its shape. Then I turned it over to them. This was training for them to develop their forearms and triceps through the repetitious downward cuts. Adam went first and was followed by Brandon. Their endurance for the cutting movements wasn't very long. Brandon accidentally cut straight down. Instead of following the round contour, he made a straight side, cutting a visible "hole" in the bush. I let the students vote whether to continue with the round contour and keep the "hole" or chop the bush down to nothing. They elected to cut it down completely. This bush was about six feet in diameter.

So they started chopping furiously. Neighbors couldn't believe their eyes. One person driving her large SUV visually locked onto the bush and its attackers. She drove looking backwards for about 20 feet. Yes, that was dangerous. My students petered out rapidly and I took over again. But this was supposed to be an exercise for them. After chopping about 80% of the bush, I ended up with painful tendonitis near my right elbow.

2001 Sunday Class – Sazzy, Jason, Brandon, Patrick, Pat, Vannak and Kaci

*

My son Brandon is always training on his own. Sometimes out of nowhere he'll start punching and kicking. Sometimes it's at me. Usually it is poor timing and I'm busy doing something and certainly not in the mood. He reminds me of Hung Wing Ding, Hung Hay Kwan's son. Brandon is playful and always wants to train. In this regard he is like a lion cub messing with his parent. The parent ready to swat him because he doesn't want to play.

Brandon Chinn   **Jason Chinn**   **Adam Lee**

My nephew Adam Lee trained at the Bellevue Kung-Fu Club briefly in 1983. At that time his sister Cori and he were a little too young for a "hard core" class. In 2002 my nephew Adam started training again with me on Sundays along with my sons. He purchased a combat weight nine ring saber and performed the form quite well. He ended up competing in Canada at Ken Low's CanAm Championships. He also demonstrated this form at the 2005 World of Martial Arts.

Jackie and Jamie in Staff Class

Jackie and Jamie Song, my step-daughters were cute and energetic. They were very bright and always did their best in class. The girls learned techniques easily and were very coordinated in the movements they practiced. I always wanted them in class, and gave them special physical activities to challenge them.

My nephew Preston just went through the summer training with me. He did a great job and learned quickly. He shows great potential and will continue to train.

My Birthday Parties

When growing up my parents always made a big deal about birthdays. This was a Chinese "thing." It was one day out of the year that I couldn't get in trouble. Punishment would be saved for the next day! Everyone usually felt special on his or her birthdays. We were celebrated for our birth and existence.

Early 1960s Birthday Party

People were genuinely happy for you. Traditionally, the respect given to Sifus was always great. So it is no surprise that the Sifu's birthday would be celebrated by all the students.

My birthday parties were always a joint celebration by students, family members and friends. Since the Kung-Fu students are in a "family system," the gatherings were close knit. At times students would bring their families also. My birthday parties also included children who participated at my community center as well as coworkers from the Parks and Recreation Department.

These birthday parties featured games and competition. Sometimes it would be water balloon "flyers up," spider walk races, balloon walks and others. Sometimes we had demonstrations so the students could show everyone how far they progressed. Other occasions had a competition of best forms.

1985 with specialty birthday cakes

1986 "Over-the-Hill" Cake

1986 Birthday with niece Melissa

I've had some pretty great Kung-Fu birthday cakes. My girlfriend Cindy had a birthday cake made with my image on top. She took a picture of me with a pair of nunchakus to a baker for the creation. The frosting "me" was a little thinner than I actually was. And with my mustache, my frosting image looked Mexican. Still it was a fine work of art!

Lori Guilfoyle was a good friend and a very talented Recreation Leader who worked with our Senior Adult Program. She taught dance exercise, arts and crafts, candy making and cake making. She did bake some outstanding cakes for my birthdays – very beautiful cakes with our Kung-Fu school symbol on them. One cake was a creative big lump of chocolate. When I first saw it I didn't know what I was. Then I noticed all the flags had names on them. All the flags were on the left side of the "chocolate lump" except one flag was on the other side and had my name on it. I finally got it. It was an "Over-the Hill" birthday cake! I was the first to reach a 30th birthday.

The Joy of Teaching

I have always enjoyed teaching. In the Chinese martial arts schools, the organization is that of a family. The Sifu is the "father." More experienced students are older brothers and sisters to the younger, newer students. It is the job of the older students to assist in the development of the newer students, like older siblings help nurture younger ones. This is a huge contrast from a "military" type environment found in other schools and cultures.

I have always enjoyed seeing the progression of my students' skill and knowledge. I can see their joy in their accomplishments. This builds pride and self-confidence.

It seems that my greatest joy in teaching in recent years was my experience with the children of the International District/Chinatown Community Center. It is the smallest community center in the city of Seattle, in the lowest income neighborhood in this city. This community center serves a large immigrant population. Many of the participants do not have the resources to have cable television or Internet access.

Many of the young children are first or second generation Chinese. The children frequently come from very conservative homes and the parents are often always working. They usually don't have many activities to keep them busy, so they head home after school. Since I grew up going through the very same pattern, working with these children was very rewarding for me. I was able to let these children experience things that I never did as a child.

Initially I saw these children come to the community center without knowing what we did in public recreation or what to expect. As they grew more comfortable with us, we involved them in activities like basketball, table tennis, Internet usage, network gaming, Halloween Carnivals, Spring Candy Hunts and Winter Holiday Parties. We even had Lunar New Year activities. Though I programmed these numerous activities, I believe the Teen Kung-Fu Program was the best for them.

Teen Kung-Fu was a unique class, originally started as a teen program class. I saw a need to bring in the pre-teens and taught all the children together. I had never had a youth class with students ranging from 6 years old to 18 year olds. Usually children polarize towards their own age group, but not in this class.

This class was a great example of a Chinese "family" organization. The older teens were able to do most things better than their young counterparts, but the little ones could be surprisingly flexible and do some pretty amazing kicks. The younger students usually looked at the teenagers like helpful, nice older brothers. I always kept a close eye on everyone. From the beginning everyone understood that I demanded respect and a positive environment.

The older teens never treated the younger students as "second class citizens," but helped them whenever needed. The "family organization" could be readily seen whenever I split up the group to compete against each other. Sometimes the competitions were for the best horse stance, kicks, nunchaku technique or four foot staff technique. At other times it could be a light sparring game. Regardless of the activity, all the children learned to respect each other and work together.

Children started coming from other parts of town also. I thought this was great because children were getting used to diversity in the expanding group. Everyone still learned to work together and have mutual respect.

Pre-show Demonstration at the 2007 World of Martial Arts

The children worked hard and had fun. They built strength and coordination, while also developing self-esteem and confidence. I had this group of talented children perform as the pre-event demonstration at the 2007 World of Martial Arts. The group itself showed a wide range of age and diversity.

With their friends and families in the audience, the children did a great demonstration. The audience was surprised as the group effectively performed basic punching and kicking drills. I was very proud of them. More important, they were proud of themselves.

"Those that can do. Those that can't teach." HOGWASH!!!!

It has been said that "those that can do and those that can't teach." Nothing can be further from the truth. When we speak of athletics even dance, those young participants are the ones who can do the competitions. Their longevity in the competition arena is usually short-lived. Still, we must examine physical ability versus knowledge versus teaching ability.

One might be able to perform at a high competitive level for only a relatively short time. Does this individual also have the depth of knowledge to actually improve the knowledge of others in the same activity? Does this individual have the ability to engage and teach others?

The ability to perform at a high level does not mean this individual has the knowledge to teach or even the ability to explain concepts and techniques. I think people can truly progress when they have depth of understanding and the ability to teach. This knowledge is invaluable. It is the only way. A martial art, is an art. Without deeper knowledge it is merely street fighting and brawling. A person can do this for a while until they get slower and less physically fit. Knowledge is the key to being effective.

Yee Jong Pai Seizing

Teaching Workshops

Throughout the years I have taught numerous Women's Self Defense workshops. Occasionally, I have had a student with prior martial arts training. Sometimes they were black belt level. My workshops gave students the chance to learn through my personal teaching methods. They learned Chinese martial arts with effective ways to defend and defeat an opponent using the tools that they have.

Thinking differently is what made our women's self defense methods so effective. I taught things contrary to the common women's self defense techniques that are actually based on men's Karate techniques. Without years of training, it is difficult to develop techniques that are powerful enough, accurate enough and strong enough. My classes did not confuse sports martial arts with effective combat techniques.

*

In keeping with the concept of a "family organization," I have avoided teaching Kung-Fu workshops to the general public over the years. I taught my workshops to few outsiders in order to keep my techniques for my students – my family. I have only taught techniques to those that would honor where their new knowledge came from. I expected they would not pass it off as their techniques or techniques from their style.

The Satisfaction of Appreciation

The fundamental need for recognition and appreciation is needed everywhere in our daily lives. From the simplest "thank you" to the grandest displays of appreciation and recognition, we need this to confirm the worthiness of what we do and who we are. Essentially, this is respect. We need this in every relationship we have. Whether between significant others, supervisors and subordinates, parents and children or masters and their students, the qualities of recognition and appreciation need to flow both ways.

Behind Every Great Man There's a Great Woman

As I mentioned, Cindy Goto started out as my student in the summer of 1974 and eventually became my girlfriend. She was a talented martial artist and we did everything together from Kung-Fu to fishing and hunting.

Cindy was good at Kung-Fu. She was left handed with good speed and power. At any moment she would spar with me. Her skill was with the front, side and roundhouse kicks. Her best hand techniques were her back fist and step punch. She was attractive but tough!

Once I sparred with her at her parents' house in their living room. We kicked and punched on the shag carpet. Both of us wore platform shoes. I threw an outside crescent kick that hit her thumbnail. It broke off cleanly at the tip of her thumb. I immediately stopped, hugged her and apologized. She said she was okay and was not hurt. She stared at her thumb - "wowed" that the thumbnail broke off so fast and in a straight line.

Another time we were sparring at my Kung-Fu school at Columbia City on Rainier Avenue. She was so cute and beautiful. I smiled and giggled as she tried to hit me with a barrage of kicks and punches. Suddenly she got mad. Cindy said: "I may never get as good as you. Most people can't, but don't you laugh at me!" Her cuteness turned into fire. She let me know that she wanted to be taken seriously. She was right. I learned humility from her.

She would drive down with me to Puyallup where I taught at the South Hill Kung-Fu Academy. She was always a great student and other students followed her example. I noticed an unspoken competition between the owner's wife Nancy and Cindy. The intensity between both women increased, especially during sparring. That was interesting to me.

A Kung-Fu Master's Journey　　　　　　　　　　　　　　　　　　　　　　© 2009 Allen J. Chinn

I had a problem with some Franklin High School gangsters. These guys tried crashing a college Halloween party I was at and all of a sudden I was their target. As long as there were five or more of them, they yelled at me with bravado. But in smaller numbers they would sheepishly walk away without a whimper.

One day five of them were in the hallway and acted like they were going to attack me. The lunch bell rang and they said I was lucky. So I went upstairs and asked a few friends and asked if they would back me up. They agreed. When the little gangsters saw us, they ran like the cowards that they were. I drove away with Cindy, but my car drove very "bumpy." That is when I noticed that they had flattened my tire.

The next day after I dropped off Cindy, one of her friends warn me that two carloads of the little gangsters showed up with older ones. They brought guns, knives, bats and pipes. I thanked the concerned friend. Then I drove up to Cleveland High School and asked my brother and a few of his friends if they would back me up. They were in. We took off to Franklin. I didn't want to fight, but if it came down to it I was ready to take any of or all of them one on one. I just wanted people to back me up, in case they attacked me with numbers.

With our group there at Franklin, the five antagonists became scared. They didn't have their older friends there. So they made up a story that it was my brother that stated it by saying something negative. They were lying little weasels. Security was afraid that there was going to be a small riot, but I shook their hand and left in peace. To ensure this situation would no longer continue, or escalate Cindy made a few phone calls. She spoke to Ruby Chow, a prominent member of the King County Council who used her community connections to quiet things down.

Cindy and I would go to watch Kung-Fu exhibitions that were new events in the mid-1970s. I was 19 years old. At one exhibition I saw a great Kung-Fu performer. His cat stance bow was very flashy. Later I mimicked his energetic, exaggerated salute. Cindy saw what I was doing and told me not to be "too cocky" and to remain humble. I thought about it and quickly cut it out.

Cindy was wonderful. She even took the second week off from her family vacations to be back with me for my birthdays. She was always there for me. She worked hard to win my mother over. This was quite a challenge because Cindy was Japanese American and my mother had gone through the Japanese occupation of China during World War II. Cindy set up a dinner for my mother to met her Chinese stepfather, and Japanese mother. Cindy and my mother became very close, even with the inability to communicate with each other. Even after Cindy and I were no longer together, she and my mother exchanged Christmas cards and gifts for many years.

*

Connie Mitchell and I started dating in 1978. Our friends had set us up on a blind date. In a whirlwind romance, we married a year later. When we first started dating, we talked about our hobbies and things we liked to do. I told her I was a Kung-Fu instructor and that one day she should visit my class. At the time I was teaching a private class of about eight students at my parents' house. She and her friend Jana stopped by to visit and that was the first time she actually saw me perform Kung-Fu techniques. We laughed later when she found out how good I was. She said: "I thought you were just another Asian guy that thought he knew martial arts!"

During her pregnancy in late 1979, we discussed what to name our child. We went over all sorts of names and even purchased a book to assist us in naming "baby" Chinn. There was no Internet back then! One night while driving home, we talked about what our child would be great at. As typical expectant parents, we were excited about the future of their child.

I said: "Our child will be the best martial artist!" Connie jumped in and said: "We'll send him to the best instructor!" I paused. Slowing and softly I stated: "I am the best instructor." Connie replied: "I know you're good, but I mean the best instructor." I left this one alone.

Later when discussing how my martial arts style developed, she did not believe that I could learn basics from my father and then create a style on my own. She related her experience with ballet and thought it was impossible to have so much knowledge and ability, without first having a lengthy experience in a well established martial arts school. She later found out that with the success of my students in tournaments and my demonstrations, I had achieved what seemed impossible.

My son Jason was born the following summer. I continued to have private students. By the fall of 1980 I had opened a small Kung-Fu school in Kent. We had 15 to 20 students. Half of the students were my gun customers of mine from Auburn Sports and Marine. Connie decided to take classes from me at that point, thinking Kung-Fu was more practical than ballet. Instead of regular Kung-Fu uniforms, we wore navy blue warm ups, with white stripes and my symbol silk screened on the chest.

Connie was supportive throughout my martial arts career. She took numerous pictures. She collected everything into photo albums and scrapbooks. Without her efforts the pictures would have been lost forever. Though we had major differences, she was always supportive of my martial arts and was a good Sifu's wife. She put up with years of my private students coming to our home. For years she drove out to Canadian tournaments and sat through all those long events and exhibitions. She was wonderful.

Most Severe Kung-Fu Injury

One day at the Columbia City school, I was working on high side kicks with Darryl Easter's help. We didn't have any sophisticated equipment and we lacked a focus pad. So Darryl used his hand as my target for throwing high right side kicks. With his hand about six feet high, I threw a couple of side kicks and tapped his hand. When I threw another side kick, he flinched and moved his hand, raising it to about six and a half feet. As I watched his hand and instinctively tracked the moving target, my foot flew upward to the new height. I suddenly heard a loud pop and then felt a ripping sensation from my left buttock, down to the back of my knee. I was in excruciating pain. I had to stop moving and sit down.

In those days no one knew anything about sports medicine. I hobbled in tremendous pain everywhere I walked. I worked at Jafco, on Westlake Avenue in the Sporting Goods Department. Our stock was in the nearby warehouse. We had to pull our own items when the customers were ready to purchase them. For three days, I walked like Quasimodo. This was no exaggeration.

Back at the Kung-Fu school, I could only kick waist height with my right side kick. So I used the injury as an opportunity to train my left side kick to be as high as the right one was. Both sides were fairly close, but with my injury, I could now only focus on the left side. As bad luck would have it, another student flinched as I was kicking his hand with a left high side kick. For next few months I could only side kick waist high with either side.

20 years later I had pain and soreness in my left hamstring. I was certain that I didn't do anything to damage it. Somehow the old injury came back. It was not near as painful and I remembered, but it was uncomfortable. I laid off Kung-Fu and basketball for a while. With rest it healed.

10 years after that, I happened to be dating a massage therapist. One day I was fortunate enough to receive a massage from her. As she was working on my hamstrings, she stated that there was a bunch of scar tissue there. She worked on it, trying to break the scar tissue down. I was amazed that she could feel the scar tissue. I didn't know that was possible.

Unforeseen Benefits of Kung-Fu

High level of coordination from training in Kung-Fu hand movements and weaponry led me to be successful in a large variety of sports as an adult including competitive basketball, volleyball and table tennis. I attribute the strength, speed, reflexes, accuracy of movement and coordination to my Kung-Fu training.

In basketball I have been a good three point shot over the years. I also excelled in defense. I used my strength and coordination developed from Kung-Fu, to be an effective backup center on my team. I have been able to use my strength and balance to defend against 6' 5" big men.

In volleyball, my speed and reflexes have been my assets. Often I dive for the volleyball intentionally. But there are numerous times I've done diving digs purely instinctive reactions.

In table tennis I am known for heavy spins, defense and quick reflexes. My playing style is unorthodox. I look like I'm using a double-edged straight sword, or fighting knife when trying to create spin at various angles. My blocking is reminiscent of step punching. My thinking and strategy give me an edge. I study other playing styles and use tactics to overcome their apparent strengths. This sounds familiar doesn't it?

Grief

We never know what life deals to us. Neither I nor anyone else could have ever imagined my successes in my career, martial arts, firearms and parenting. However, life is like the Yin and Yang. For every space of good, there also occupies the same amount of space for the bad. The good and bad, happy and sad are all a balance in life. The forces of Yin and Yang are not opposing forces. They should be viewed as complimentary. One cannot exist without the other.

So I have also had my share of grief and sadness. I have had devastating losses in my life. I never thought I would have had to endure a divorce, let alone two. It was very difficult to end those relationships. I had invested all my emotions; my desires and my future in them. It was devastating to abruptly stop those feelings of love and belonging and to lose the life I was living.

*

The passing of my parents was very difficult to deal with as well. My life was built on the support of my parents. My early lessons in life and upbringing were all due to the care and love I received from them. I owe so much to them.

When my sister and I met the pastor for my mother's funeral, we spent a little time discussing my mother and her background. He later related to us that when he lost his last surviving parent, he suddenly realized he was an orphan. I actually felt better before he made that statement.

Like Star Wars when characters see the spirits of those that meant the most to them, I sometimes see my parents. I remember their lessons and what they used to say to me. These vivid memories can be very emotional sometimes and bitter sweet. But they are invaluable to me.

My parent through the years

Another type of grief and loss is the growing up of my sons. It is hard to stop the amount of caring and support that I had given them from birth. My life took a different path because of my desire to be there for them. My sons and I have always been close. Their challenges in life were my challenges too. Whether it was tough projects from school, challenging homework or their efforts in sports, I was always there to support them. I was there at the hospital with them, whether it was due to a car accident, an assault or a health concern.

2000 with my parents

Three Brothers 2007

Though we remain close, they are adults now. My involvement in their daily lives has been reduced. Thus, I suffer from the "empty nest syndrome." They have their own hopes and dreams. I still worry about them. This I learned from my mother.

Extended Family

I have my family and relatives and then I have a wonderfully large number of extended family members. I love my family. I feel love and concern for my extended family as well. Over the years I have had numerous students that because of the Chinese "family organization" in my martial arts have been the main source of my "other" family.

I have also had numerous friendships and relationships that blossomed into knowing that these amazing people were really "family" to me. I cannot imagine a world without these fine individuals who mean so much to me.

*

Some time ago I gave my top students a "Chinn" sweatshirt for Christmas. It was heavy, had black material and a large red Chinese character for my surname. One day Rich Brady and Shawn Miller were in Chinatown to take Cantonese lessons. While they were walking an old Chinese man stopped Shawn and looked at his sweatshirt. He stated "You're a Chinn, I'm a Chinn!" They all laughed and then parted.

What We Are Today is the Product of What We've Experienced in the Past

I've written about my beginnings and experiences. I truly believe that everything we are today was influenced by what we experienced in our past. Decision making, upbringing, past behavior, external influences, friendships, relationships, responsibilities, beliefs, positive and negative events, good luck and bad luck - all play in shaping who and what we are.

We should have an understanding that martial arts and life are a combination of everything around us. Everything touches us in some way.

In 1989 I was touched by the generosity of my students. For my Christmas present they purchased a custom engraved Detonics Combatmaster MK I, 45 acp pistol.

I thought about them and made a videotape of our Jong Hop Kune form for each of them. I also told them:

"Life is like a small pond. The water is still and calm. Each of us are like small pebbles. When we are tossed into the calm waters of the pond, we create small ripples ever expanding. Each ripple touches another. You have touched my life and I thank you."

We should find learning and understanding in the innumerable influences and contacts we all have.

1988 Eastside Karate Association Tournament Demonstration with Michael Gibson

A Kung-Fu Master's Journey

© 2009 Allen J. Chinn

Scrapbook articles: 1974 Beacon Hill News, 1981 Auburn Globe News, 1983 International Examiners, 1984 West Seattle Herald, 2007 International Examiner

Could You Have Ever Imagined

Shawn Miller and I were talking about our martial arts a couple of years ago and I asked: "Could you have ever imagined in your wildest dreams that you would be teaching Kung-Fu in Chinatown one day?" Shawn smiled and said that this was something he could never have imagined. It would be highly unlikely for a Black Sifu to be teaching in a closed network where few Kung-Fu schools existed. In fact it would be difficult for anyone to teach in an environment where old traditions are still observed and territories are still guarded.

We never really know what we will become. Life is full of twists and turns and we never know what will lead us to the people or events that change our fate.

 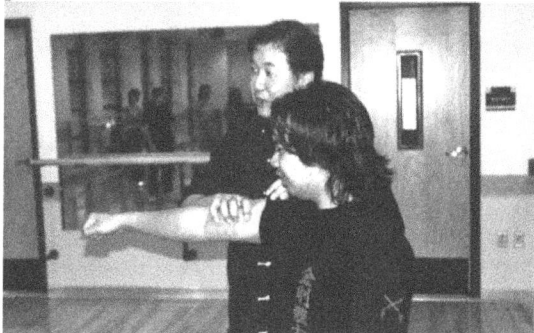

2005 Women's Self Defense Workshop

The Future of Yee Jong Pai

The future of Yee Jong Pai Kung-Fu lies in the capable hands of Shawn Miller. Over the years he has been that amazingly high quality clay that I have worked with. When I'm gone I know he will be the very accomplished master potter. I am proud of him. He has been everything a Kung-Fu master would want in a student.

Shawn Miller, me and David Thanphilom   **Sifu Shawn Miller**

Retired in 2009

Mrs. Leong, wife of Grandmaster John Leong, saw me at Ken Low's 30th Can-Am Championships held in British Columbia in May. She seemed surprised to see me. I greeted her and her husband and she said: "I heard you retired!" I smiled and responded that my retirement was with the City of Seattle but not from Kung-Fu.

My retirement came as quite a surprise for most people who knew me. For most of my 24 2/3 years as a supervisor with the Seattle Department of Parks and Recreation I have been happy. I was content with my work with the public. I always felt my contributions to the communities I served in very rewarding.

However, I felt that I had too much tenure to be a victim of bigotry and prejudice. I felt that I could no longer work with an organization whose decision makers had no people skills nor management skills. I enjoyed working with the majority of the people I've known throughout the years. Though few, the people who used anything to climb the bureaucratic ladder or to keep their superiors happy became too much for me to endure.

As a retired person, I am now free to complete the book and DVD projects I have had on a back shelf over the years. Actually my first book project started 35 years ago. Life and its many bumps and curves delayed my writing until now.

My son Brandon thought about my situation and came to the conclusion that I'm picking up where I left off 35 years ago. He stated that I get to go back to what I was doing before work, career, marriages and children happened. Brandon then asked would my book have been better back then, or now. I stated that back then all I wanted to do was write an instructional book on my personal style of Kung-Fu. Now I have much more knowledge and understanding. There are scores of books I could write on the various aspects of Kung-Fu, self defense and combat.

I remember a statement from Bruce Friedman about 20 years ago. "When you quit are you going to open up a school? You were born to teach!"

I will teach privately, write my books and film my DVDs and de-stress.

My Journey

I have not reached the end of my journey. No doubt there will be new chapters in my life and new teachings to be taught. There are new things I hope to learn and experience. This book is actually a check point and a review of how I got to this stage of my life.

The end of my journey will be with my last breath. The final destination is the goal that we don't want to reach because the journey is what adds color to our lives. Hopefully this final destination will be in the far future but we never know what is next to come. When that time comes, I hope to be remembered for being a great martial artist, firearms expert, great teacher, great mentor, multi-talented, great father, great relative, great friend and a good person. This is more than I could have ever imagined.